1600+ Fascinating Facts!

1648 MIND-BOGGLING FACTS: HISTORY, MUSIC, NATURE, PEOPLE, SCIENCE, SPORT, TECHNOLOGY, THE UNIVERSE, AND ALL THAT LIES BETWEEN!

MAX MERCURY

Copyright © by Max Mercury/CleverClick Press
All rights reserved.
No part of this publication may be reproduced, distributed, or transmitted in any form or by any means, including photocopying, recording, or other electronic or mechanical methods, without the prior written permission of the publisher, except in the case of brief quotations embodied in critical reviews and certain other noncommercial uses permitted by copyright law.

ISBN: 9798854462372

First Edition: 2023

CleverClick Press
275 New North Road
London
N1 7AA
United Kingdom

CleverClickPress.com

For permissions, inquiries, or general correspondence regarding this book, contact the publisher at the above address or via email at info@cleverclickpress.com.

Table of Contents

Introduction	1
Technology and Innovation	**3**
Amazon Marketplace	3
Artificial Intelligence	5
Cryptocurrency	7
Cybersecurity	9
Driverless Technology	11
Drone Technology	13
Facebook	15
Incredible Engineering Feats	17
Inventors and their Inventions	19
Revolutionary Technology	21
Streaming Services	23
The Gig Economy	25
The Internet	27
Virtual Reality	29
Nature and Wildlife	**31**
African Wildlife	31
Animal Kingdom	33
Birds of the World	35
Botany and Plant Life	37
Dinosaurs	39
Endangered Species	41
Insects and Bugs	43
Mammals of the World	45
Natural Disasters	47
Ocean Life	49
Reptiles and Amphibians	51
The Universe	**53**
Constellations	53
Space Travel	55
The Solar System	57
The Universe and Beyond	59
UFO's	61
Art and Literature	**63**
Art and Artists	63
Books and Literature	65

Classical Ballet	67
Classical Literature	69
Famous Authors	71
Famous Paintings	73

History and Exploration — 75
Explorers and Expeditions	75
Famous Architects	77
Famous Astronomers	79
Famous Battles	81
Famous Bridges	83
Famous Buildings	85
Famous Castles	87
Great Leaders in History	89
Greek Mythology	91
Historic Events	93

Anatomy — 95
Human Evolution	95
Human Psychology	97
The Human Body	99

People — 101
Barack Obama	101
Bill Gates	103
Donald Trump	105
Elon Musk	107
Greta Thunberg	109
Kim Jong-un	111
Mark Zuckerberg	113
Meghan Markle	115
Pope Francis	117
Prince Harry	119
Queen Elizabeth II	121
Vladimir Putin	123

Science — 123
Famous Scientists	125
Genetics and DNA	127
Geology and Rocks	129

Human Society and Culture — 131
Festivals and Celebrations	131
Food and Nutrition	133
Global Cultures	135
Human Rights	137

Influencers	139
Native American Cultures	141
Social Media	143
Strange Country Laws	145
Women's Rights	147
World Cuisines	149
World Languages	151
World Religions	153
Sports and Entertainment	**155**
Sports Around the World	155
Sports Legends	157
Sportsmanship and Fair Play	159
The FIFA World Cup	161
The Olympics	163
The Premier League	165
The Superbowl	167
The Environment	**169**
Climate Change	169
Earthquakes	171
Energy Sources	173
Peculiar Weather Phenomena	175
Plastic Pollution	177
Renewable Energy	179
Volcanoes	181
Wildfires	183
Ancient Civilization	**185**
Ancient China	185
Ancient Egypt	187
Ancient Greece	189
Ancient India	191
Ancient Rome	193
Music	**195**
Famous Composers	195
Musical Genres	197
Musical Instruments	199
The World	**201**
World Currencies	201
World Flags	203
World Maps	205
World Oceans	207
World Records	209

World Time Zones	211
Social Topics	**213**
Black Lives Matter	213
COVID-19	215
North Korea	217
Miscellaneous	**219**
Amazing Coincidences	219
Mathematics and Numbers	221
Mythical Creatures	223
Strange Phobias	225
Unexplained Disappearances	227
Unknown Movie Facts	229
Unsolved Mysteries	231
About the Author	**233**
Inspire Our Next Edition	**235**

Introduction

Welcome to the world of *'1600+ Fascinating Facts!'*—a fact book that will tickle your curiosity, ignite your imagination, and leave you brimming with mind-boggling knowledge!

In these pages, you'll encounter the wonders of modern marvels like Artificial Intelligence, Driverless Technology, and Virtual Reality. Unleash your inner tech geek and discover the secrets behind revolutionary inventions that shape our world.

But wait, there's more! We'll dive deep into the wild wonders of African Wildlife and explore the diverse creatures inhabiting the Animal Kingdom. From the magnificent Mammals of the World to the tiniest Insects and Bugs, our natural world will dazzle you with its boundless beauty.

Prepare to have your mind blown by the thrilling accounts of Legendary Sports Figures, the pulse-pounding excitement of global events like The Olympics and The FIFA World Cup, and the fascinating tales of triumph and sportsmanship.

And that's just the tip of the iceberg! From the quirkiest World Records to the enigmatic realms of Unsolved Mysteries, from the delightful peculiarities of World Cuisines to the pressing challenges of Climate Change and Plastic Pollution, this fact book is a treasure trove of knowledge.

So, buckle up, fellow fact enthusiasts! Let's embark on an unforgettable quest through the realms of wisdom, where facts become legends and learning becomes an adventure!

Amazon Marketplace

1. Amazon's original name was "Cadabra," but it was changed to "Amazon" because CEO Jeff Bezos wanted a name that started with the letter "A" to appear at the top of alphabetical lists.

   "From books to billions!"

2. The company initially only sold books when it launched in 1994. The first book ever sold on Amazon was titled "Fluid Concepts and Creative Analogies" by Douglas Hofstadter.

3. Amazon's logo was designed to represent a smile that goes from A to Z, symbolizing the variety of products available on the platform.

4. The Kindle e-reader, introduced by Amazon in 2007, revolutionized the publishing industry and popularized e-books. It quickly became one of the company's most successful products.

Technology and Innovation

5. Amazon Prime, the company's subscription-based service, launched in 2005 and initially offered free two-day shipping. It has expanded to include additional benefits like streaming services and exclusive deals.

"Dog food made history!"

6. The first item ever ordered through Amazon Prime was a large bag of dog food in 2005.

7. Amazon acquired the popular streaming platform Twitch in 2014 for approximately $970 million, entering the live streaming and gaming market.

8. Amazon's fulfillment centers are massive, with some exceeding one million square feet in size. The largest one, located in Illinois, covers over 2.4 million square feet.

9. Amazon has expanded its business beyond online retail, venturing into industries such as grocery stores with the acquisition of Whole Foods Market in 2017.

10. Amazon Go, the company's chain of cashier-less convenience stores, allows customers to grab items and leave without having to go through a traditional checkout process.

11. In 2018, Amazon became the second company to reach a market valuation of $1 trillion, following Apple's achievement earlier that year.

12. Amazon's CEO, Jeff Bezos, briefly surpassed Bill Gates as the world's richest person in 2017 and held the position for several periods.

13. The company's annual shopping event, Prime Day, was first held in 2015 to celebrate Amazon's 20th anniversary. It has since become a highly anticipated global sales event.

"1.3 million employees and counting!"

14. As of 2021, Amazon employed over 1.3 million people worldwide, making it one of the largest employers globally and a significant driver of job creation.

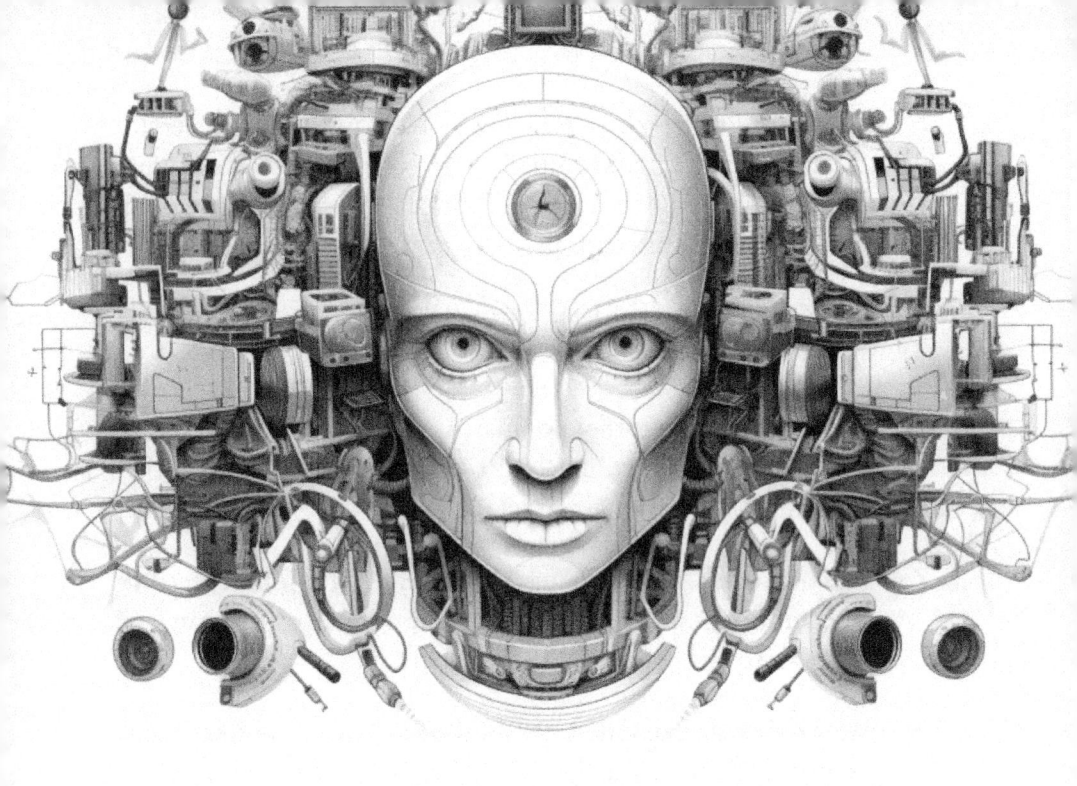

Artificial Intelligence

1. AI can accurately diagnose certain medical conditions better than human doctors, such as identifying skin cancer from images.

2. In Japan, an AI program named Lulubot is being used to offer emotional support to individuals facing mental health issues.

3. Researchers have developed AI algorithms that can create art, compose music, and even write poetry that is nearly indistinguishable from human-created works.

4. The AI program DeepMind defeated world champion Go player Lee Sedol, showcasing the immense progress made in AI's strategic thinking abilities.

    "Language ninjas at your service!"

5. AI-powered virtual assistants like Siri, Alexa, and Google Assistant use natural language processing to understand and

"AI: The backseat driver we all need!"

respond to user commands.

6. AI is used in autonomous vehicles to enhance safety and efficiency, enabling features like adaptive cruise control and lane-keeping assistance.

7. AI algorithms have been used to develop robots capable of performing intricate surgical procedures with enhanced precision.

8. AI-powered language translation services like Google Translate utilize neural networks to provide accurate and contextually relevant translations.

9. AI is being employed in the energy sector to optimize power grids, reduce energy consumption, and facilitate the integration of renewable energy sources.

"Saving the planet one pixel at a time!"

10. AI algorithms can analyze satellite imagery to track deforestation, monitor wildlife populations, and aid in environmental conservation efforts.

11. AI is transforming the field of cybersecurity by identifying and preventing cyber threats in real-time, safeguarding networks and sensitive data.

12. AI-powered drones are being used for tasks such as search and rescue operations, agricultural monitoring, and infrastructure inspections.

13. AI algorithms can analyze human facial expressions to detect emotions, leading to applications in market research, psychology, and social robotics.

14. AI is assisting in drug discovery and development by predicting the efficacy and side effects of potential medications, accelerating the research process.

Cryptocurrency

1. Satoshi Nakamoto, the anonymous creator of Bitcoin, remains unknown, and their true identity continues to puzzle the cryptocurrency community.

2. The first real-world transaction using Bitcoin occurred in 2010 when someone bought two pizzas for 10,000 Bitcoins.

    "That's 300 Million USD!"

3. Bitcoin mining consumes a significant amount of energy, with estimates suggesting that it consumes more electricity than entire countries.

4. The supply of Bitcoin is limited to 21 million coins, making it a deflationary currency that cannot be inflated by central banks.

5. The total market capitalization of all cryptocurrencies combined surpassed $2 trillion for the first time in April 2021.

Technology and Innovation

6. Cryptocurrency wallets are not physical wallets but software programs that store private keys necessary to access and manage cryptocurrencies.

7. Initial Coin Offerings (ICOs) are a fundraising mechanism used by blockchain projects to raise capital by issuing their own tokens.

8. Bitcoin is divisible up to eight decimal places, and the smallest unit of Bitcoin is called a satoshi, named after its mysterious creator.

"El Salvador loves El Bitcoin!"

9. Some countries, like El Salvador, have adopted Bitcoin as legal tender, making it the first nation to officially recognize a cryptocurrency.

10. The pseudonymous nature of blockchain transactions provides a certain level of privacy, but it is not entirely anonymous.

11. The concept of stablecoins emerged to address the issue of price volatility, with these cryptocurrencies pegged to stable assets like fiat currencies or commodities.

12. The first cryptocurrency ATM was installed in Vancouver, Canada, in 2013, enabling users to exchange Bitcoin for cash and vice versa.

"Slow and steady wins the race!"

13. The transaction speed of the Bitcoin blockchain is relatively slow, with an average block time of around 10 minutes.

14. The environmental impact of cryptocurrencies has led to the rise of eco-friendly alternatives like Proof-of-Stake (PoS) blockchains, which consume significantly less energy compared to Proof-of-Work (PoW) systems.

Cybersecurity

1. The first known computer virus, "Creeper," was created in 1971 and spread through ARPANET, the predecessor of the Internet.

2. A "honeypot" is a cybersecurity technique where a decoy system is set up to lure hackers and gather information about their methods.

3. The term "phishing" originates from the word "fishing" and describes the practice of tricking individuals into revealing sensitive information through fraudulent emails or websites.

4. Stuxnet, a sophisticated worm discovered in 2010, was designed to sabotage Iran's nuclear program by targeting industrial control systems.

    "When worms go nuclear!"

5. The world's first cyberattack occurred in 1988 and was known

Technology and Innovation

"Blocking the internet, one byte at a time!"

as the "Morris Worm," which infected approximately 6,000 computers.

6. The "Great Firewall of China" is a complex system of internet censorship that restricts access to certain websites and online content within China.

7. Cybersecurity professionals often use "white hat," "black hat," and "gray hat" to categorize hackers based on their intentions and actions.

8. "Keyloggers" are malicious programs that record a user's keystrokes, allowing hackers to capture sensitive information like passwords and credit card details.

9. The majority of cyberattacks are financially motivated, with hackers seeking to steal money, valuable data, or personal information for financial gain.

10. "Two-factor authentication" (2FA) adds an extra layer of security by requiring users to provide two different forms of identification to access an account.

11. A "botnet" is a network of compromised computers infected with malware, allowing hackers to control them remotely for various malicious purposes.

12. The "Heartbleed" bug, discovered in 2014, exposed a critical flaw in OpenSSL, a widely used cryptographic library, potentially compromising millions of websites.

"Battle of the geeks!"

13. "Cyberwarfare" involves nation-states engaging in offensive and defensive operations in cyberspace to gain advantages or disrupt the activities of other countries.

14. The "Kill Chain" model is a framework used in cybersecurity to describe the stages of a cyberattack, from initial reconnaissance to the final objective.

Driverless Technology

1. The concept of driverless technology dates back to the 1920s, when radio-controlled cars were showcased at science fairs.

2. The first fully autonomous vehicle was built in the 1980s by Carnegie Mellon University, nicknamed the "Navlab."

    "Beer delivery reaches peak efficiency!"

3. In 2016, an autonomous truck completed the first-ever commercial delivery, transporting 50,000 cans of beer in Colorado.

4. Autonomous taxis are expected to become a widespread mode of transportation, potentially reducing the need for individual car ownership.

5. Self-driving cars can communicate with each other, sharing information about road conditions, traffic, and potential hazards.

Technology and Innovation

"Like buses, but without the grumpy drivers!"

6. Driverless shuttles have been deployed in various cities worldwide, offering efficient and eco-friendly transportation options for short distances.

7. Autonomous vehicles can adapt their driving style based on traffic conditions, weather, and the preferences of their occupants.

8. Some companies are experimenting with the idea of using self-driving vehicles to deliver packages and goods, enhancing logistics operations.

9. Driverless technology has the potential to transform the trucking industry, reducing costs and improving efficiency in long-haul transportation.

10. Artificial intelligence algorithms play a crucial role in autonomous vehicles, allowing them to interpret sensor data and make driving decisions.

11. Self-driving cars are equipped with redundant systems to ensure safety, including backup sensors, multiple computers, and fail-safe mechanisms.

"Saving the planet one mile at a time!"

12. Autonomous vehicles can analyze vast amounts of data to optimize fuel efficiency, reducing greenhouse gas emissions and promoting sustainability.

13. Driverless technology faces challenges in handling complex traffic scenarios, adverse weather conditions, and the unpredictability of human drivers.

14. The legal and regulatory frameworks surrounding autonomous vehicles are being developed to address liability, privacy, and safety concerns in the future.

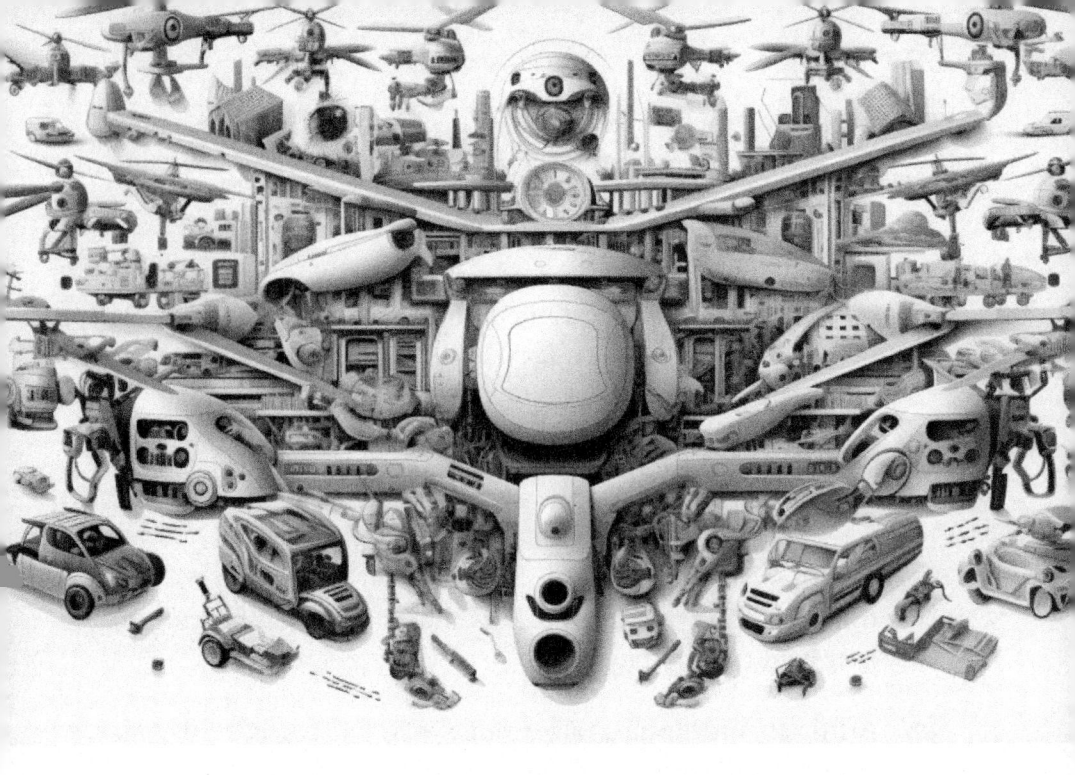

Drone Technology

1. The smallest commercially available drone, the "Piccolissimo," weighs just 2.5 grams and fits in the palm of your hand.

2. In 2016, a drone called the "Super Drone" set a Guinness World Record by lifting a 61.6 kg payload, showcasing its incredible lifting capabilities.

3. Drones can be equipped with thermal imaging cameras to detect heat signatures and locate missing persons or wildfires.

4. The world's fastest drone, the "RacerX," reached a top speed of 163.5 mph (263.7 km/h) in 2017. *"Usain Bolt's distant cousin!"*

5. In 2020, a drone named "Ingenuity" made history by being the first aircraft to achieve powered flight on another planet, Mars.

Technology and Innovation

"Drones to the rescue!"

6. Drones have been used in conservation efforts to monitor wildlife populations, track poaching activities, and protect endangered species.

7. Drone swarms, where multiple drones work together in a coordinated manner, are being explored for various applications, including search and rescue missions.

8. The world's largest drone delivery network is being developed in Rwanda, where drones transport medical supplies to remote areas.

"Bee-saving superheroes in disguise!"

9. In Japan, drones have been employed to pollinate flowers in areas where declining bee populations pose a threat to agriculture.

10. Some drones are designed to fly for extended periods using solar panels, making them more sustainable and environmentally friendly.

11. Drone technology is being integrated with 3D printing to create innovative construction techniques, such as autonomous bricklaying.

12. Drones have been used to inspect and maintain infrastructure, such as bridges and power lines, reducing the need for dangerous manual inspections.

13. The military uses drones for surveillance, reconnaissance, and targeted strikes, significantly enhancing their operational capabilities.

14. Drones are revolutionizing the film industry, allowing filmmakers to capture stunning aerial shots previously only possible with expensive helicopter setups.

Facebook

1. Facebook was initially called "The Facebook" when it launched in 2004, exclusively for Harvard students, before expanding to other colleges.

2. The iconic "Like" button was almost named "Awesome" or "Awesome" button, but Mark Zuckerberg ultimately settled on "Like."

   "Innovate or hack off!"

3. A "Hacker Way" sign hangs in Facebook's headquarters, symbolizing the company's culture of encouraging employees to be bold and innovative.

4. The famous "Poke" feature, initially intended as a friendly gesture, sparked widespread confusion among users, leading to its gradual decline.

5. The "Blue Bar of Death" was an internal term used for

Technology and Innovation

"Facebook's BFF!" — Facebook's signature blue error page shown during site outages.

6. In 2012, Facebook acquired Instagram for $1 billion, a move that proved pivotal in maintaining its social media dominance.

7. In 2013, Facebook went dark for 30 minutes due to a server error, leading to a temporary plunge in global web traffic.

8. The company hosts a yearly event called "Hacktober" to promote coding and hackathon-style projects among its employees.

9. The "Social Graph" refers to the intricate web of connections between users, enabling Facebook to personalize content and ads.

10. In 2009, a bug caused private messages to be displayed publicly on users' Facebook walls, causing privacy concerns.

11. "Facebook Addiction Disorder" is a psychological term used to describe excessive use and dependency on the platform.

12. Facebook experimented with "Facebook Credits," a virtual currency used for virtual goods in games, but discontinued it in 2013.

13. The company introduced the "On This Day" feature in 2015, allowing users to see their past Facebook activity on a specific date.

"Bullying, beware!"

14. Facebook's "Compassion Research Day" encourages researchers to study and promote positive online interactions, aiming to combat cyberbullying and negativity.

Incredible Engineering Feats

1. The Panama Canal, an extraordinary engineering marvel, spans 48 miles and allows ships to cross between the Pacific and Atlantic Oceans, saving them from a treacherous journey around South America.

2. The International Space Station (ISS) is a stunning example of collaboration between 15 nations. It orbits Earth at a speed of 17,500 mph and completes one revolution every 90 minutes.

3. The Burj Khalifa in Dubai stands as the tallest man-made structure in the world, soaring to a height of 2,722 feet. Its construction involved 330,000 cubic meters of concrete and 39,000 tons of steel.

4. The Channel Tunnel, connecting the United Kingdom and France, stretches for 31 miles beneath the English Channel. It

"Europe's underwater shortcut!"

features the longest underwater portion of any tunnel in the world, at 23.5 miles.

5. The Three Gorges Dam in China is the world's largest hydroelectric power station, generating a mind-boggling 22,500 megawatts of electricity and reducing carbon emissions by millions of tons each year.

6. The Hubble Space Telescope, positioned 340 miles above Earth, has provided breathtaking images of distant galaxies since its launch in 1990. Its discoveries have revolutionized our understanding of the universe.

"Windy, shaky but iconic!"

7. The Golden Gate Bridge in San Francisco is an iconic symbol of engineering prowess. It spans 1.7 miles and endures extreme weather conditions, including strong winds and frequent earthquakes.

8. The High-Speed Rail (HSR) network in Japan is renowned for its efficiency and punctuality. It operates at speeds of up to 200 mph, allowing commuters to travel quickly between major cities.

9. The Great Wall of China, an astonishing feat of engineering, stretches over 13,000 miles and was built to protect China from invasions during ancient times. It is a UNESCO World Heritage site.

10. The Shanghai Maglev Train in China employs magnetic levitation technology, allowing it to reach speeds of 267 mph. It's the fastest commercially-operating train in the world.

"Battle of the geeks!"

11. The Akashi Kaikyo Bridge in Japan is the longest suspension bridge in the world, spanning 6,532 feet. It withstands powerful earthquakes and typhoons, showcasing exceptional engineering resilience.

Inventors and their Inventions

1. The invention of the microwave oven was accidental. Percy Spencer, an engineer, discovered it when a chocolate bar in his pocket melted while he was working on a magnetron.

2. The inventor of the television, Philo Farnsworth, first conceived the idea at the age of 14 while plowing a field. He sketched out the concept of electronic television in the soil.

3. The inventor of the computer mouse, Douglas Engelbart, initially called it a "bug." The first prototype was a wooden shell with two metal wheels that tracked movement.

   "The unsung heroes of fasteners!"

4. Velcro was inspired by burrs. Swiss engineer George de Mestral noticed how burrs clung to his dog's fur during a walk, leading to the creation of the famous hook-and-loop fastener.

5. The light bulb was not solely invented by Thomas Edison.

Technology and Innovation

While Edison developed a practical version, the incandescent light bulb's concept was actually invented by Sir Joseph Swan, a British physicist.

6. The inventor of the telephone, Alexander Graham Bell, considered his greatest invention to be the photophone, which transmitted sound on a beam of light before the invention of the telephone.

7. Wilhelm Roentgen discovered X-rays accidentally while experimenting with cathode rays. He noticed a glow on a nearby fluorescent screen and realized he had discovered a new type of radiation.

8. Benjamin Franklin did not invent electricity, but he conducted extensive experiments on it. His famous kite experiment demonstrated the connection between lightning and electricity.

9. The inventor of the World Wide Web, Sir Tim Berners-Lee, originally proposed the concept as a way for scientists to share information efficiently within the research community.

"A sandy stroke of genius!"

10. The barcode was invented by Norman Woodland and Bernard Silver, who developed the concept while sitting on a Miami beach, drawing lines in the sand and imagining a system for automatic product identification.

11. The first practical revolver, the Colt Paterson, was invented by Samuel Colt. He designed a revolving cylinder that enabled rapid firing, revolutionizing firearms technology.

12. The inventor of the Segway, Dean Kamen, had originally envisioned it as a wheelchair that could climb stairs, but it eventually became a popular personal transportation device.

"Proving naysayers wrong, one change at a time!"

13. The inventor of the disposable diaper, Marion Donovan, initially faced resistance from manufacturers. They believed parents wouldn't buy something they would throw away, but her invention proved them wrong.

Revolutionary Technology

1. In the realm of revolutionary technology advancements, scientists have developed a self-healing material that can repair itself when damaged, mimicking the regenerative abilities of living organisms.

   "Math's wild, mysterious cousin!"

2. Quantum computing, an emerging field, harnesses the principles of quantum mechanics to perform complex computations at unparalleled speeds, potentially revolutionizing fields such as cryptography and optimization.

3. Researchers have developed smart contact lenses capable of measuring glucose levels in tears, offering a non-invasive approach to monitoring blood sugar levels for individuals with diabetes.

4. The development of printable electronics has paved the way

Technology and Innovation

for flexible displays, allowing screens to be rolled up or bent without compromising their functionality.

5. The emergence of brain-computer interfaces enables direct communication between the human brain and computers, opening up possibilities for controlling devices using only our thoughts.

6. 3D bioprinting has made significant strides, allowing scientists to create functional human organs using a combination of living cells and specialized bio-inks.

"The superheroes of cleanliness!"

7. Advancements in nanotechnology have led to the creation of self-cleaning surfaces, where tiny nanoparticles prevent dirt and bacteria from adhering to the material.

8. Scientists have developed ultra-thin, transparent solar cells that can be integrated into windows, enabling buildings to generate electricity while still allowing natural light to pass through.

9. Advances in machine learning and artificial intelligence have enabled the development of self-driving cars, which hold the potential to significantly reduce traffic accidents and transform transportation systems.

"Putting Picasso out of business!"

10. Scientists have made progress in creating artificial intelligence systems capable of generating creative works, such as music, paintings, and even writing original stories.

11. In the field of renewable energy, solar panels are becoming more efficient and cost-effective, driving the adoption of clean energy sources and reducing reliance on fossil fuels.

12. Virtual reality (VR) technology immerses users in simulated environments, offering realistic experiences in fields such as gaming, training, and therapy.

Streaming Services

"Making '90s kids feel ancient!"

1. Streaming services initially gained popularity in the late 2000s, but the concept of streaming media dates back to the 1990s.

2. The first streaming service, known as NetFlix, was launched in 1997. Initially, it only offered DVD rentals by mail.

3. Netflix revolutionized the way TV shows are produced by introducing the concept of releasing entire seasons at once, known as "binge drops."

4. In 2020, streaming services accounted for 82% of all TV viewing time in the United States, surpassing traditional cable and satellite TV.

5. Streaming services collect vast amounts of user data, which helps them personalize recommendations and improve their content libraries.

"Rest in peace, rewind fees!"

6. The rise of streaming services led to the decline of video rental stores, such as Blockbuster, which filed for bankruptcy in 2010.

7. The success of streaming services paved the way for the rise of original content, with platforms like Netflix and Amazon producing award-winning TV shows and movies.

8. The world's largest streaming service is YouTube, with billions of users streaming videos on the platform every day.

9. As streaming services continue to grow, there is an ongoing battle among platforms to secure exclusive rights to popular shows, resulting in fierce competition.

"Clogging the internet, one show at a time!"

10. The popularity of streaming services has led to an increase in internet traffic, causing concerns about the strain on network infrastructure.

11. The first film to win an Academy Award for Best Picture and be primarily distributed through a streaming service was "Parasite" in 2020.

12. Some streaming services offer offline viewing, allowing users to download and watch content later without an internet connection.

13. The emergence of streaming services has given rise to a phenomenon called "spoiler culture," where viewers must be cautious about discussing shows to avoid revealing spoilers.

14. Streaming services have become global powerhouses, expanding their reach to multiple countries and offering localized content to cater to diverse audiences worldwide.

The Gig Economy

1. The term "gig economy" was coined in 2009 and refers to a labor market characterized by short-term, flexible jobs.

2. The gig economy is estimated to comprise about 34% of the U.S. workforce, with over 57 million people participating.

3. Platforms like Uber, Lyft, and Airbnb popularized the gig economy by connecting workers directly with consumers.

    "Work from home, bed, or beach!"

4. Gig workers often enjoy the freedom to choose their own hours and work locations, providing a greater work-life balance.

5. Despite its benefits, gig work is often precarious, with limited job security and benefits like health insurance and retirement plans.

6. The gig economy has expanded into various sectors beyond

Technology and Innovation

transportation and accommodation, including freelance writing, graphic design, and consulting.

"Still rocking the side hustle!"

7. Gig workers have diverse backgrounds, ranging from students and freelancers to retirees and individuals seeking supplemental income.

8. Research shows that gig workers often experience higher job satisfaction levels than traditional employees.

9. Gig workers may face challenges in terms of income volatility and difficulties in accessing loans or mortgages due to the lack of traditional employment contracts.

10. Some argue that gig workers should be classified as employees to ensure they receive appropriate benefits and protections.

11. The rise of technology has enabled gig platforms to efficiently match workers with consumers, optimizing convenience for both parties.

"Turning hobbies into serious business!"

12. Gig work has given rise to a new breed of entrepreneurs who leverage their skills and resources to create successful businesses.

13. The gig economy has sparked innovation in payment systems, with digital platforms providing seamless and instant transactions.

14. As the gig economy continues to evolve, policymakers and stakeholders are working to strike a balance between flexibility and worker protection.

The Internet

1. The first-ever email was sent in 1971 by Ray Tomlinson, who used the @ symbol to separate the user from the host.

2. The term "spam" for unwanted emails originated from a Monty Python sketch where the word was repeated excessively.

   "The origin of spam!"

3. The first-ever YouTube video was uploaded on April 23, 2005, titled "Me at the zoo" by Jawed Karim.

4. The world's first website, info.cern.ch, was created by Tim Berners-Lee and went live on August 6, 1991.

5. The Internet was originally known as ARPANET, developed by the U.S. Department of Defense for military purposes.

6. The dark web, a part of the Internet not indexed by search engines, is estimated to be several times larger than the surface

Technology and Innovation

web.

7. In 1990, the first web browser, WorldWideWeb (later renamed Nexus), was created by Tim Berners-Lee.

8. :-), the first-ever emoticon to express happiness, was used by computer scientist Scott Fahlman in an email in 1982.

9. The term "Wi-Fi" doesn't stand for anything specific. It was coined as a play on "Hi-Fi" (high fidelity) for marketing purposes.

"6 hours and 42 minutes avoiding productivity!"

10. The average person spends around 6 hours and 42 minutes online every day, according to a 2021 report by We Are Social.

11. The Internet is estimated to have over 5 billion users worldwide, representing approximately 60% of the global population.

12. The concept of a "viral video" originated from a Nike advertisement featuring Ronaldinho that spread rapidly across the Internet.

"Clickbait before clickbait!"

13. The first-ever banner ad was launched in 1994 and had a click-through rate (CTR) of 44%, significantly higher than current rates.

14. The term "meme" was coined by Richard Dawkins in his 1976 book "The Selfish Gene" to describe cultural ideas spreading online.

Virtual Reality

1. Virtual Reality (VR) technology was initially developed for flight simulators in the 1960s to train pilots and create realistic simulations.

2. The term "virtual reality" was coined by Jaron Lanier in the late 1980s, who is often referred to as the "father of virtual reality."

3. The first consumer VR headset, called the Virtual Boy, was released by Nintendo in 1995 but failed to gain widespread popularity due to its monochromatic display and discomfort during use.

   "Where reality takes a coffee break!"

4. VR arcades have become popular in many cities, allowing people to experience high-quality VR experiences without investing in expensive equipment.

Technology and Innovation

5. VR can be used for more than just gaming and entertainment; it has been utilized in fields such as medicine, education, architecture, and military training.

6. The Oculus Rift, a pioneering VR headset, gained attention through its successful Kickstarter campaign in 2012, raising over $2.4 million in funding.

7. Similar to motion sickness, VR sickness can occur when there is a disconnect between the motion perceived in VR and the body's actual motion, leading to nausea and dizziness.

8. The haptic feedback technology in VR allows users to feel touch and sensations in virtual environments through the use of specialized gloves, suits, or controllers.

9. In 2016, the first VR feature film, "Jesus VR - The Story of Christ," was released, allowing viewers to experience the narrative as if they were present in the scenes.

10. The military uses VR extensively for training purposes, enabling soldiers to simulate combat scenarios, practice tactics, and improve decision-making skills.

    "The future of 'ouchless' procedures!"

11. VR is being explored as a tool for pain management, with studies showing that immersive experiences can help reduce pain perception and distraction during medical procedures.

    "The next best thing to a DeLorean!"

12. VR technology has been employed in museums and historical sites to recreate ancient civilizations and enable visitors to explore and interact with historical artifacts.

13. Architects and designers use VR to create virtual walkthroughs of buildings and spaces, allowing clients to experience and make changes before construction begins.

14. The film industry has embraced VR by creating 360-degree videos and immersive storytelling experiences that transport viewers into the heart of the action.

African Wildlife

1. The African elephant is the largest land mammal and can communicate through low-frequency vibrations that can travel several kilometers.

   "The original tree-hugger!"

2. The African leopard is a master of stealth and can drag prey more than twice its body weight up into a tree to avoid competition from other predators.

3. The Cape buffalo, also called the African buffalo, is considered one of the most dangerous animals in Africa due to its unpredictable and aggressive nature.

4. The Goliath frog, native to Equatorial Guinea and Cameroon, is the largest frog species in the world, with some individuals growing up to 32 centimeters (12.6 inches) long.

5. The African penguin, found along the coastlines of South

Nature and Wildlife

Africa and Namibia, is the only species of penguin that breeds in Africa.

6. The African lungfish, able to survive in both water and mud during dry periods, can aestivate for up to four years by burying itself underground.

7. The shoebill stork, native to East Africa, has a distinctive shoe-shaped bill and is known for its patient, statue-like behavior while hunting for fish.

"The champion of long, slithery hugs!"

8. The African rock python is one of the largest snake species in the world, capable of reaching lengths of over 6 meters (20 feet).

9. The baobab tree, found throughout Africa, has a massive trunk and can store up to 120,000 liters (32,000 gallons) of water during the dry season.

10. The African civet, a nocturnal mammal, secretes a strong musk-like scent called civetone, which has been used to produce perfumes for centuries.

11. The African fish eagle, often considered the voice of Africa's waterways, has a distinct call that resembles the sound of a high-pitched, echoing laugh.

12. The aardvark, meaning "earth pig" in Afrikaans, is not a pig at all but a nocturnal mammal that feeds mainly on ants and termites.

13. The aardwolf, a small, insectivorous mammal, has specialized teeth and a long, sticky tongue that it uses to feed almost exclusively on termites.

14. The African grey parrot, known for its exceptional intelligence and mimicry abilities, is one of the most popular pet bird species worldwide.

"Grey parrots: Einstein's feathered friends!"

Animal Kingdom

1. The largest animal kingdom on Earth is home to an estimated 8.7 million species, but scientists believe over 90% are still undiscovered.

2. The pistol shrimp possesses a unique claw that creates a bubble capable of reaching temperatures hotter than the sun's surface.

   "The DJ of the deep!"

3. The blue whale, the largest animal known to have existed, can produce sounds that travel over 1,000 miles underwater.

4. The unique mimic octopus found in the waters of Southeast Asia can imitate the appearance of various marine animals to avoid predators.

5. The bombardier beetle has a defense mechanism that involves mixing two chemicals inside its body, resulting in a boiling, toxic explosion.

"The underwater boxing champion!"

6. The mantis shrimp has the fastest punch in the animal kingdom, reaching speeds comparable to a bullet fired from a .22 caliber gun.

7. The axolotl, also known as the "Mexican walking fish," can regenerate lost body parts, including limbs and even parts of its heart and spinal cord.

8. The vampire finch, another resident of the Galapagos, has developed a taste for blood and feeds on the blood of other birds by pecking at their skin.

"Living fossil or slime superhero?"

9. The hagfish, often called a "living fossil," has remained virtually unchanged for the past 300 million years and produces slime as a defense mechanism.

10. The blue poison dart frog is one of the most toxic animals on Earth, with its skin containing enough poison to kill up to 20,000 mice.

11. The star-nosed mole has a highly sensitive snout with 22 fleshy appendages that allow it to detect prey faster than the human eye can follow.

12. The red-lipped batfish in the Galapagos has adapted to walk on the ocean floor using its modified pectoral fins.

13. The Kakapo, a flightless parrot native to New Zealand, is the heaviest parrot species in the world and has a strong nocturnal nature.

14. With its distinctive large nose, the saiga antelope can filter out dust during dust storms and regulate its body temperature in extreme conditions.

Birds of the World

1. The African grey parrot is known for its exceptional intelligence, capable of understanding and mimicking human speech with astonishing accuracy.

2. The hummingbird is the only bird capable of flying backward, thanks to its unique wing structure and rapid wing beat of up to 80 times per second.

   "Who needs a plane with wings like those?"

3. The wandering albatross has the largest wingspan of any living bird, reaching up to 11.5 feet (3.5 meters) long.

4. The male superb lyrebird from Australia is an amazing mimic, able to replicate not only other bird calls but also sounds like car alarms and chainsaws.

5. The Secretary bird of Africa has long legs that it uses to stomp on its prey, such as snakes, to immobilize them before

Nature and Wildlife

swallowing them whole.

"That's one heck of a round trip!"

6. The Arctic tern undertakes the longest migratory journey, traveling an average of 44,000 miles (71,000 kilometers) round trip from the Arctic to the Antarctic and back each year.

7. The kea, a parrot species native to New Zealand, is known for its mischievous behavior, including stealing shiny objects from hikers and damaging car windscreen wipers.

8. The barn owl has exceptional hearing, with heart-shaped facial discs that help to channel sound to their ears, allowing them to locate prey in complete darkness.

9. The red-billed quelea, found in Africa, is the most abundant bird species on Earth, with an estimated population of over 1.5 billion individuals.

10. The peregrine falcon is the fastest bird in level flight, capable of reaching speeds of over 240 miles per hour (386 kilometers per hour) during hunting dives.

"Batman's distant cousin!"

11. The oilbird, found in South America, is the only nocturnal fruit-eating bird in the world, using echolocation to navigate in complete darkness.

12. The African fish eagle, also known as the "voice of Africa," has a distinctive call often associated with African wildlife documentaries.

13. The male penduline tit, found in Europe and Asia, constructs an intricately woven hanging nest, which swings like a pendulum to deter predators.

14. The male weaverbirds are skilled architects, constructing elaborate nests made of woven grass and plant fibers, often hanging from branches and swaying in the wind.

Botany and Plant Life

1. The corpse flower (Amorphophallus titanum) produces the largest unbranched inflorescence in the world, reaching heights of up to 10 feet.

    "The drama queen of plants!"

2. Mimosa pudica, also known as the sensitive plant, folds its leaves when touched, a defense mechanism against herbivores.

3. The bristlecone pine (Pinus longaeva) is one of the oldest known living organisms, with some individuals exceeding 5,000 years in age.

4. The Welwitschia plant from Namibia has only two leaves that grow continuously throughout its lifespan, which can exceed 1,000 years.

5. The largest living thing on Earth is a honey fungus (Armillaria ostoyae) in Oregon, covering an area of over 2,385 acres.

Nature and Wildlife

6. Pitcher plants have adapted to carnivory by trapping and digesting insects in their pitcher-shaped leaves to obtain nutrients.

7. The quaking aspen (Populus tremuloides) forms massive colonies of genetically identical trees connected by a single root system.

8. The seeds of the African tulip tree (Spathodea campanulata) have wings, enabling them to be dispersed by wind over long distances.

9. The resurrection plant (Selaginella lepidophylla) can survive extreme dehydration and "come back to life" when water is available again.

10. The Saguaro cactus (Carnegiea gigantea) can live for over 150 years and doesn't start growing its first arm until it reaches the age of 75.

11. The quinine tree (Cinchona pubescens) produces quinine, a compound used to treat malaria.

"A plant with a 'killer' instinct!"

12. The Venus flytrap (Dionaea muscipula) uses trigger hairs on its leaves to sense and capture insects for nutrition.

13. The agave plant takes several decades to flower, and when it does, it shoots up a massive inflorescence that can reach up to 40 feet in height.

"The ultimate sun chasers!"

14. Some plants, like the sunflower, exhibit heliotropism, meaning they track the sun's movement throughout the day.

Dinosaurs

"The tiny dinosaur with big dreams!"

1. The smallest known dinosaur, the Microraptor, was about the size of a crow and had wings capable of flight.

2. Dinosaurs ruled the Earth for over 160 million years, more than 15 times longer than humans have existed.

3. The fastest dinosaur, the Ornithomimus, could reach up to 40 miles per hour.

4. The first dinosaur fossil discovered was an incomplete megalosaurid thigh bone found in England in 1676.

5. The Stegosaurus had a brain the size of a walnut, making it one of the least intelligent dinosaurs.

6. Some dinosaurs, such as the Ankylosaurus, had armor-like plates and bony spikes on their bodies for defense.

Nature and Wildlife

7. Not all dinosaurs were giants; some were as small as chickens, like the Compsognathus.

"The original chicken nugget!"

8. The oldest known dinosaur eggs were discovered in Argentina and date back to around 231 million years ago.

9. The Argentinosaurus, one of the largest dinosaurs, may have weighed up to 100 tons, making it heavier than a Boeing 737.

10. Some dinosaurs, like the Velociraptor, had sharp, curved claws on their hind legs that they likely used to hunt and kill prey.

"The coolest place for dino parties!"

11. Dinosaurs lived on all continents, including Antarctica, although it was not always covered in ice during the Mesozoic Era.

12. The Triceratops had a frill on its head that could grow up to 6 feet long and may have been used for display or defense.

13. The bite force of the T. rex is estimated to be one of the strongest among all animals, exerting pressures of up to 8,000 pounds per square inch.

14. The extinction of non-avian dinosaurs occurred around 66 million years ago, likely due to a combination of factors, including an asteroid impact and volcanic activity.

Endangered Species

1. The axolotl, a Mexican salamander, can regenerate lost limbs, organs, and even parts of its spinal cord.

2. The vaquita, a rare porpoise found in the Gulf of California, is the most endangered marine mammal, with less than 10 individuals remaining.

3. The Philippine tarsier has the largest eyes in proportion to the body size of any mammal and can rotate its head nearly 180 degrees.

    "The real unicorn we need!"

4. The saola, often called the "Asian unicorn," is one of the rarest large mammals and was only discovered by scientists in 1992.

5. The red panda is not closely related to giant pandas and has a false thumb, which helps it grasp bamboo and climb trees.

Nature and Wildlife

"A rare ball of fluff!"

6. The northern hairy-nosed wombat is one of the world's rarest mammals, with less than 250 individuals living in a single location in Australia.

7. The Iberian lynx is the world's most endangered wild cat species, with fewer than 100 individuals remaining in Spain and Portugal.

8. The pangolin is the most trafficked mammal in the world due to the high demand for its scales and meat.

9. The Chinese giant salamander is the largest amphibian in the world, reaching lengths of up to six feet.

10. The gharial, a crocodile species in India and Nepal, has an extremely thin, elongated snout adapted for catching fish.

11. The Hawaiian monk seal is one of the rarest marine mammals and is endemic to the Hawaiian Islands.

12. The white rhinoceros is the second-largest land mammal after the elephant and is distinguished by its square upper lip.

"Laying eggs like a boss!"

13. The kiwi, a flightless bird native to New Zealand, lays one of the largest eggs in proportion to its body size.

14. The Ethiopian wolf, also known as the Simien fox, is the rarest canid species and is found only in the Ethiopian highlands.

Insects and Bugs

1. Insects and bugs make up over 80% of all known animal species on Earth, with estimates ranging from 6 to 10 million different species.

   "That's one big bug!"

2. The largest insect in the world is the Goliath beetle, which can reach lengths of up to 4.5 inches and weigh as much as 3.5 ounces.

3. Honeybees have a remarkable ability to communicate with each other through complex dances, informing other bees about the location of food sources.

4. Dragonflies are incredibly agile fliers and can change direction mid-flight, fly backward, and hover in one spot due to their exceptional wing control.

5. The lifespan of adult mayflies can be as short as a few minutes,

Nature and Wildlife

with some species living for just a few hours, making them one of the shortest-lived insects.

6. Beetles are the largest group of insects, comprising approximately 25% of all known animal species on the planet.

7. The fastest recorded flying insect is the horsefly, which can reach up to 90 miles per hour (145 kilometers per hour).

"Nature's camouflage artists!"

8. Stick insects, also known as walking sticks, are masters of disguise and can mimic twigs or leaves to blend in with their surroundings.

9. Some species of fireflies synchronize their flashing patterns to attract mates, creating mesmerizing light displays in certain regions.

10. The termite is considered the most successful decomposer on Earth, breaking down dead plant material and recycling nutrients back into the ecosystem.

"Small but mighty!"

11. The smallest known insect is the fairy wasp, with females measuring only about 0.14 millimeters in length.

12. Some species of ants engage in a practice known as "slavery" by raiding and capturing the pupae of other ant species to serve as workers in their own colonies.

13. The caterpillar of the gypsy moth has tiny hooks on its feet that allow it to crawl upside down and even across smooth glass surfaces.

14. Insects have been used in various medical research, such as studying their ability to regenerate limbs and exploring their potential in wound healing.

Mammals of the World

1. The blue whale, the largest mammal on Earth, has a heart the size of a small car and can weigh up to 2,000 pounds (907 kg).

2. Bats are the only mammals capable of sustained flight, using their elongated fingers to form wings and navigate through the air.

    "The original wingmen!"

3. The cheetah, known for its incredible speed, can accelerate from 0 to 60 mph (97 km/h) in just a few seconds, making it the fastest land mammal.

4. The echidna, a spiny anteater, is one of only two egg-laying mammals in the world alongside the platypus.

5. Narwhals, often called the "unicorns of the sea," have long tusks that can grow up to 10 feet (3 meters) in length.

Nature and Wildlife

"Proof that size matters!"

6. Elephants are the largest land mammals, with the African elephant standing up to 13 feet (4 meters) tall and weighing around 12,000 pounds (5,443 kg).

7. Dolphins are highly intelligent mammals and have been observed using tools like sponges to protect their noses while searching for food.

8. The polar bear is the largest bear species and has adapted to life in the Arctic, with a thick layer of blubber and a white fur coat.

9. The quokka, a small marsupial found in Australia, is often referred to as the world's happiest animal due to its perpetually smiling face.

10. The sugar glider, a small possum native to Australia and New Guinea, has a membrane called a patagium that allows it to glide between trees.

"The tiny monkeys that rule!"

11. The pygmy marmoset, or the finger monkey, is the smallest monkey species, with adults weighing around 3.5 ounces (100 grams).

12. The numbat, a small marsupial native to Western Australia, primarily feeds on termites and can eat up to 20,000 termites in a single day.

13. The red kangaroo is the largest marsupial and can reach up to 40 mph (64 km/h) while hopping across the Australian outback.

14. Meerkats, small mammals native to southern Africa, have a complex social structure and live in tight-knit groups called mobs or clans.

Natural Disasters

1. Lightning strikes during thunderstorms can generate temperatures of up to 30,000 degrees Celsius, making them hotter than the sun's surface.

2. The largest earthquake ever recorded occurred in Chile in 1960, with a magnitude of 9.5 on the Richter scale.

3. Tsunamis can travel up to 800 kilometers per hour (500 miles per hour) in the open ocean, but slow down as they approach shore.

"Nature, giving Earth a chill pill!"

4. A volcanic eruption can release millions of tons of ash into the atmosphere, causing a temporary cooling effect on the Earth's surface.

5. Hurricanes, cyclones, and typhoons are all names for the same type of storm, but they are called differently depending on the

Nature and Wildlife

region they occur in.

6. The deadliest natural disaster in history was the 1931 China floods, which claimed the lives of an estimated 2-4 million people.

7. Tornadoes can produce wind speeds of over 300 miles per hour (480 kilometers per hour) and leave a trail of destruction in their wake.

8. The Great Red Spot on Jupiter, a massive storm, has been raging for at least 300 years and is larger than the Earth.

9. Sinkholes can form when underground water dissolves certain types of rocks, causing the ground above to collapse.

10. Mudslides, also called debris flows, occur when a mass of soil, rock, and water rapidly moves downhill, often with devastating consequences.

"Earth's version of a messy downhill race!" (note on item 10)

11. Due to the intense heat and airflow, wildfires can create their own weather systems, including pyrocumulus clouds and fire whirls.

12. Avalanches are rapid downhill movements of snow, ice, and debris, often triggered by snowstorms or human activity in mountainous regions.

13. The Richter scale, used to measure earthquake magnitudes, is logarithmic, meaning that a one-unit increase represents a tenfold increase in ground shaking.

"Where shaking goes logarithmic!" (note on item 13)

14. The "thunder snow" phenomenon occurs when thunder and lightning accompany heavy snowfall, creating a unique combination of winter weather and electrical activity.

Ocean Life

1. The humpback whale, known for its beautiful songs, can communicate with other whales up to 1,000 miles away through its melodic melodies.

2. The pistol shrimp is an incredible creature that generates a sound louder than a gunshot by snapping its claw shut, stunning its prey.

3. The immortal jellyfish has the unique ability to revert back to its juvenile form after reaching adulthood, effectively restarting its life cycle.

4. The mantis shrimp possesses the fastest punch in the animal kingdom, capable of striking with the speed of a bullet. *"Toothbrush shopping must be a nightmare!"*

5. The Pacific Viperfish has long, needle-like teeth that are so large it can't even close its mouth.

Nature and Wildlife

6. The chambered nautilus, a distant relative of squid and octopuses, has a stunning spiral-shaped shell and can live up to 20 years.

7. The blue tang fish, known for its bright colors, can change its hue depending on its mood or environment.

8. The giant clam can weigh up to 500 pounds and live for over 100 years, making it one of the longest-lived animals on Earth.

9. The snapping shrimp uses its powerful claw to create a cavitation bubble, which releases a shockwave that can stun or kill prey.

10. The leafy sea dragon, resembling a floating seaweed, is a master of camouflage, blending seamlessly into its surroundings.

    "Dad of the Year award right there!"

11. The male seahorse carries the fertilized eggs in a pouch until they hatch, making them one of the few animals where males bear offspring.

12. Despite its ominous name, the vampire squid is a gentle creature that feeds mainly on marine snow, organic particles falling from above.

13. The barotrauma phenomenon occurs when deep-sea fish brought to the surface rapidly experience their swim bladder expanding, causing their eyes to bulge.

    "The DJ of the ocean!"

14. The blue whale, the largest animal ever known to have existed, can produce sounds that travel thousands of miles underwater, aiding in communication and navigation.

Reptiles and Amphibians

1. The tuatara, a reptile native to New Zealand, has a "third eye" on top of its head to detect light and dark.

2. The Gharial, a critically endangered crocodilian species, has the most slender snout of any living crocodilian.

   "Now that's what I call a snout!"

3. Some amphibians, like the axolotl, can regenerate entire limbs, spinal cords, and even parts of their heart and brain.

4. The Chinese soft-shelled turtle can respire through its rear end, using specialized blood vessels in its cloaca to extract oxygen from water.

5. The Gaboon viper, found in central and western Africa, has the longest fangs of any venomous snake, measuring up to 2 inches (5 cm) in length.

6. The poison dart frog is one of the most toxic animals on Earth, with some species possessing enough venom to kill 10 adult humans.

7. The flying gecko has developed a remarkable adaptation called "gliding," allowing it to effortlessly glide through the air using flaps of skin on its body.

8. The Komodo dragon, the largest lizard on Earth, has venomous saliva that helps it bring down its prey by inducing shock, paralysis, and blood loss.

"A lizard with a built-in detachable tail!"

9. The spiny-tailed iguana, native to Mexico, can break off its tail as a defense mechanism and later regrow a replacement.

10. The green anaconda is the heaviest snake in the world, capable of reaching lengths of over 25 feet (7.6 meters) and weighing up to 550 pounds (250 kg).

11. The Indian purple frog spends most of its life underground and only emerges for a short period each year during the monsoon season to breed.

12. The horned lizard has the unique ability to shoot blood from its eyes as a defense mechanism against predators.

"The living X-ray of the jungle!"

13. The glass frog's translucent skin allows its internal organs, including its heart, liver, and digestive tract, to be visible from the outside.

14. The olive ridley sea turtle exhibits an incredible phenomenon known as "arribada," where thousands of females simultaneously come ashore to lay their eggs.

Constellations

"Cassiopeia: The cosmic alphabet soup!"

1. The constellation Cassiopeia is shaped like a "W" or "M" and contains the famous "Bubble Nebula," an enormous interstellar cloud.

2. Orion, known for the three iconic belt stars, is home to the Orion Nebula, one of the most active star-forming regions.

3. Taurus holds the Pleiades, a young star cluster also known as the Seven Sisters, which can be seen with the naked eye.

4. Scorpius contains the red supergiant star Antares, approximately 700 times larger than our Sun.

5. Leo, the Lion, boasts the famous spiral galaxy Messier 66, which is part of the Leo Triplet of galaxies.

6. Auriga, the Charioteer, showcases the open star cluster Messier

The Universe

37, which is over 500 million years old.

"Flying high with cosmic bling!"

7. Pegasus, the Winged Horse, is associated with the Perseus constellation and features the bright globular cluster Messier 15.

8. Centaurus, one of the largest constellations, contains Alpha Centauri, the closest star system to our Solar System.

9. Aquarius, the Water Bearer, is home to the Helix Nebula, a planetary nebula resembling a giant eye in space.

10. Sagittarius, depicted as an archer, contains the center of our Milky Way galaxy and is rich in star clusters and nebulae.

11. Gemini, the Twins, is known for the star Pollux, a giant star with a planet confirmed to orbit it.

12. Cancer, the Crab, is located near the ecliptic and contains the famous open cluster known as the Beehive Cluster.

13. Virgo, the Maiden, houses the giant elliptical galaxy Messier 87, which contains a supermassive black hole at its center.

"Our next-door spiral princess!"

14. Andromeda, named after the mythological princess, is home to the Andromeda Galaxy, our closest spiral neighbor in space.

Space Travel

"Space, the ultimate soundproof room!"

1. Space is completely silent because sound waves need a medium to travel through, and space is a vacuum.

2. Spacecraft returning to Earth can experience temperatures up to 3,000 degrees Fahrenheit due to friction with the atmosphere.

3. The Voyager 1 spacecraft, launched in 1977, has entered interstellar space and continues to send data back to Earth.

4. Astronauts on the International Space Station witness 16 sunrises and sunsets every day due to its orbit.

5. Space is not completely empty; it contains particles and gases, although they are extremely spread out.

6. Astronauts often experience "space fog" or "space brain" due

to the effects of microgravity on their cognitive abilities.

7. Astronauts have to exercise for about two hours a day to combat muscle and bone loss caused by living in microgravity.

"Orbiting the Earth like a boss!"

8. In 1962, John Glenn became the first American to orbit the Earth, completing three orbits in just under five hours.

"The ultimate space couch potato!"

9. The longest continuous stay in space by an astronaut is 437 days, set by Russian cosmonaut Valeri Polyakov.

10. The International Space Station (ISS) is the largest human-made structure in space, with a mass of over 400 metric tons.

11. A trip to Mars would take an average of 9 months, depending on the alignment of Earth and Mars in their orbits.

12. Space travel can cause changes in the shape of astronauts' eyeballs, leading to visual impairments known as space flight-associated neuro-ocular syndrome (SANS).

13. The farthest distance traveled by a human in space is 248,655 miles (400,171 km) during the Apollo 13 mission, which swung around the far side of the moon.

14. The first living beings to return from space were fruit flies aboard a U.S. V-2 rocket launched in 1947.

The Solar System

1. Mercury, the closest planet to the Sun, experiences extreme temperature differences, with surface temperatures reaching over 800 degrees Fahrenheit during the day and dropping to -290 degrees Fahrenheit at night.

2. Venus has the longest rotation period among all the planets, taking around 243 Earth days to complete one full rotation on its axis.

3. Jupiter, the largest planet in the solar system, has a colossal storm known as the Great Red Spot, which has been raging for at least 400 years.

    "Uranus, the planet that likes to show off!"

4. Uranus is a unique planet with an axial tilt of 98 degrees, causing it to essentially rotate on its side compared to other planets.

The Universe

5. Saturn's mesmerizing rings are made up of countless tiny particles, ranging in size from grains of sand to enormous chunks several meters in diameter.

6. Neptune, the farthest planet from the Sun, has the strongest winds in the solar system, reaching up to 1,300 miles per hour (2,100 kilometers per hour).

"Pluto, still the coolest dwarf in the neighborhood!"

7. Pluto, once considered the ninth planet, was reclassified as a "dwarf planet" in 2006 due to its small size and location in the Kuiper Belt.

8. The Oort Cloud is a vast and hypothetical region far beyond the Kuiper Belt, believed to be the source of long-period comets that occasionally visit our inner solar system.

9. Ganymede, a moon of Jupiter, is the largest moon in the solar system and is even larger than the planet Mercury.

10. Io, another moon of Jupiter, is the most volcanically active body in the solar system, with hundreds of active volcanoes spewing lava into space.

11. Enceladus, another moon of Saturn, has geysers erupting from its south pole, releasing plumes of water vapor and icy particles into space.

12. Mars has the tallest volcano in the solar system, Olympus Mons, which stands about three times taller than Mount Everest on Earth.

13. The Cassini-Huygens mission, a collaboration between NASA and ESA, explored Saturn and its moons, providing valuable insights into their composition and dynamics.

"Taking 'out of office' to a whole new level!"

14. The Voyager 1 spacecraft, launched in 1977, became the first human-made object to enter interstellar space, leaving our solar system behind.

The Universe and Beyond

1. The universe is estimated to be about 13.8 billion years old, and its expansion is accelerating due to a mysterious force called dark energy.

   "The universe's mysterious caffeine!"

2. The largest known structure in the universe is the cosmic web, a vast network of galaxies and intergalactic gas spanning billions of light-years.

3. Black holes are not just destroyers; they can also create. When matter falls into a black hole, it can generate intense jets of particles and energy.

4. The cosmic microwave background radiation is the afterglow of the Big Bang, detected as a faint glow of microwave radiation permeating the universe.

5. Scientists have discovered exoplanets orbiting distant stars,

including "hot Jupiters" with scorching temperatures and "super-Earths" with rocky surfaces.

"Fireworks for the cosmic stage!"

6. Stars can explode in a phenomenon called a supernova, releasing enormous amounts of energy and producing elements crucial for life, such as carbon and oxygen.

7. Neutron stars are incredibly dense remnants of massive stars. A teaspoon of neutron star material would weigh about a billion tons on Earth.

8. Dark energy, the mysterious force driving the universe's accelerated expansion, accounts for approximately 68% of the total energy in the cosmos.

"The heavyweight champion!"

9. The most massive known black hole, residing in the galaxy Holmberg 15A, has a staggering mass of 40 billion times that of our Sun.

10. Gravitational waves, ripples in spacetime, were first detected in 2015. They provide a new way to observe the universe and study cataclysmic events.

11. It is theorized that most of the universe's gold and other heavy elements are created in cataclysmic collisions of neutron stars.

12. The concept of parallel universes or a multiverse arises from various cosmological theories, suggesting the existence of other realms beyond our own.

13. There is a limit to how fast information can travel through the universe: the speed of light, which is approximately 299,792 kilometers per second.

14. The universe is not static; it is constantly evolving. Galaxies move, stars are born and die, and the cosmos undergoes a continuous cycle of change.

UFO's

1. One of the most infamous UFO incidents is the Roswell incident of 1947, where the U.S. military recovered debris from a supposed crashed UFO, sparking conspiracy theories.

2. The phenomenon known as "foo fighters" during World War II referred to mysterious aerial objects reported by Allied and Axis pilots. *"Very original, Dave!"*

3. In 1561, a mass UFO sighting occurred over Nuremberg, Germany, described as an aerial battle with strange objects in the sky.

4. Astronauts on the Apollo 11 mission reported seeing unidentified objects on their way to the moon in 1969.

5. The U.S. government's Project Blue Book, initiated in 1952, investigated over 12,000 UFO reports, with 701 remaining

"Just advanced waffle irons?" unexplained.

6. Belgium witnessed a wave of UFO sightings from 1989 to 1990, where triangular-shaped craft were spotted by thousands of witnesses.

7. The Phoenix Lights event of 1997 saw a massive V-shaped formation of lights flying over Arizona, observed by numerous witnesses, including then-Governor Fife Symington.

"Norway's rave party for orbs?"

8. The Hessdalen Lights in Norway have baffled scientists since the 1980s, with luminous, unidentified orbs appearing in the remote valley.

9. The "Wow! signal" received in 1977 from space remains unexplained, intriguing astronomers and UFO enthusiasts alike.

10. The Belgian Air Force scrambled F-16 jets to chase UFOs in 1990, capturing radar data and chasing these unknown objects across the sky.

11. An alleged UFO crash in Varginha, Brazil, in 1996 involved reports of strange creatures and intense government cover-ups.

12. The Betty and Barney Hill abduction case in 1961 was one of the first reported alien abduction incidents, garnering widespread attention.

13. Unexplained cattle mutilations often accompany UFO sightings, with reports of surgically precise incisions and missing organs in various countries.

14. Despite numerous UFO sightings and claims, there is yet no conclusive scientific evidence of extraterrestrial visitations, leaving the mystery of UFOs unsolved.

Art and Artists

"Guess van Gogh wasn't a salesperson!"

1. Vincent van Gogh, known for his striking brushwork and intense colors, only sold one painting during his lifetime.

2. Pablo Picasso, one of the most influential artists of the 20th century, created over 50,000 artworks throughout his career.

3. Michelangelo, renowned for his sculpture of David and the ceiling of the Sistine Chapel, considered himself more of a sculptor than a painter.

4. The art movement known as Dada emerged during World War I as a response to the horrors of war and embraced irrationality and absurdity.

5. The art technique of pointillism, popularized by Georges Seurat, involves creating images using small dots of pure color that blend when viewed from a distance.

Art and Literature

6. Georgia O'Keeffe, an American artist, is known for her large-scale paintings of flowers, landscapes, and skyscrapers, often with intense colors and bold compositions.

7. The art movement of Surrealism, led by Salvador Dalí and André Breton, aimed to explore the realm of the subconscious and dreams.

8. Jackson Pollock, an influential American artist, developed a unique "drip painting" style, pouring or dripping paint onto the canvas.

9. The art installation "The Gates" by Christo and Jeanne-Claude consisted of 7,503 saffron-colored fabric panels displayed in Central Park, New York City.

10. Leonardo da Vinci was not only an artist but also a scientist and inventor known for his anatomical studies and sketches of flying machines.

"Redefining art, one urinal at a time!"

11. The French artist Marcel Duchamp famously displayed a urinal as an artwork titled "Fountain," challenging traditional ideas of what constitutes art.

12. The term "impressionism" was derived from Claude Monet's painting "Impression, Sunrise," which was initially criticized but later became influential in the art world.

13. The iconic painting "The Scream" by Edvard Munch depicts a figure in distress and is seen as a symbol of existential anguish.

"Rembrandt's selfie game was on point!"

14. The Dutch painter Rembrandt van Rijn created approximately 90 self-portraits throughout his life, providing a glimpse into his evolving appearance and artistic skill.

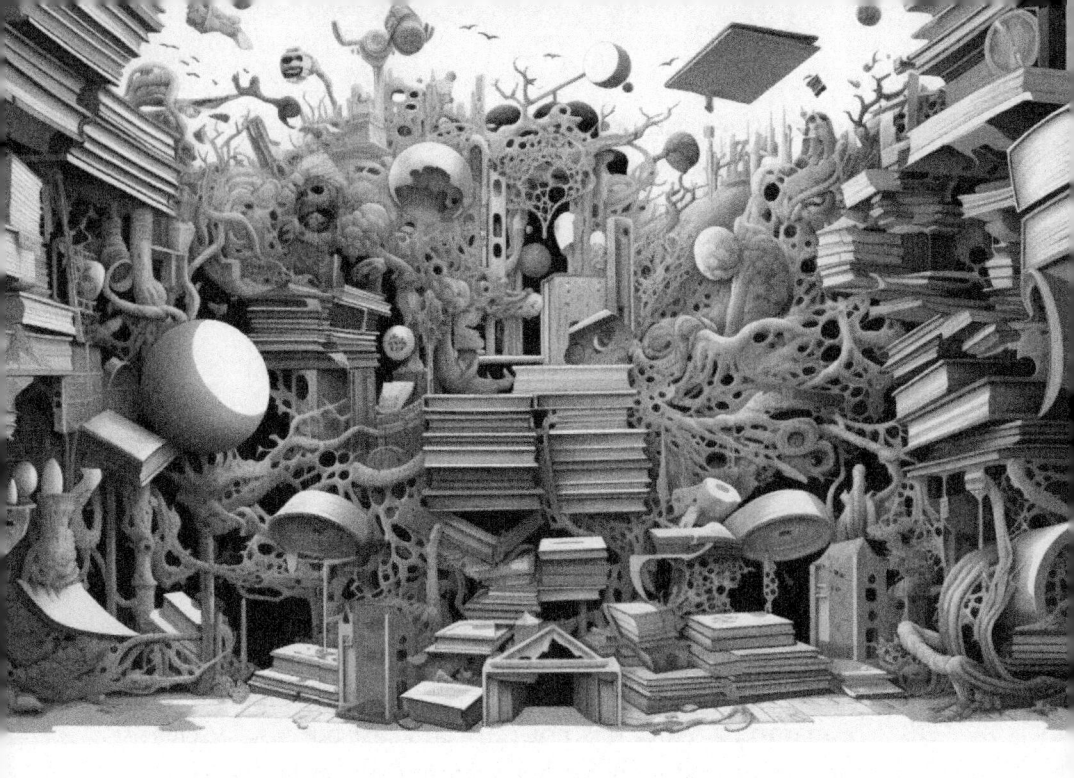

Books and Literature

1. The world's largest book is "Bhutan: A Visual Odyssey Across the Last Himalayan Kingdom," measuring 1.5 meters tall when opened.

2. The longest sentence in English literature is in Victor Hugo's novel "Les Misérables" and contains 823 words.

   "Wow, talk about starting a trend!"

3. The Tale of Genji, written by Murasaki Shikibu in the 11th century, is considered the world's first novel.

4. The Guinness World Record for the most published author of all time goes to L. Ron Hubbard, with over 1,000 published works.

5. The first known work of literature is the Epic of Gilgamesh, an ancient Mesopotamian poem dating back to the 18th century BCE.

Art and Literature

"They must be running out of shelf space!"

6. The Library of Congress, the largest library in the world, holds over 170 million items and adds approximately 12,000 items every working day.

7. Agatha Christie, the famous mystery writer, remains the best-selling novelist of all time, with over 2 billion books sold worldwide.

"Short but sweet!"

8. The shortest novel ever written is "Mickey Mouse and the Boy Thursday" by Walt Disney, which consists of only 10 words.

9. The oldest known surviving book is the Etruscan Gold Book, which dates back to the 6th century BCE.

10. The most expensive book ever sold at auction is Leonardo da Vinci's notebook "Codex Leicester," purchased for over $30 million.

11. The first book to be printed in English was "The Recuyell of the Historyes of Troye" by William Caxton in 1473.

12. The largest bookstore in the world is the Barnes & Noble bookstore in New York City, covering an area of 154,250 square feet.

13. Don Quixote by Miguel de Cervantes is widely considered the first modern novel and has been translated into more languages than any other book except the Bible.

14. The Great Library of Alexandria, once the largest library in the ancient world, was said to have housed over 700,000 scrolls before its destruction.

Classical Ballet

1. The origins of classical ballet can be traced back to the Italian Renaissance courts of the 15th century, where it began as a form of entertainment for the nobility.

2. The first ballet academy, the Académie Royale de Danse, was established in France in 1661 by Louis XIV, an avid ballet enthusiast.

3. The iconic pointe shoes, worn by ballerinas, were first developed in the early 19th century, allowing dancers to dance on their toes and create the illusion of floating.

   "The fancy ballet dictionary!"

4. Ballet terms, such as plié, arabesque, and pas de deux, are derived from the French language, reflecting the strong influence of French ballet on the art form.

5. The Nutcracker, one of the most famous ballets, was initially

considered a failure when it premiered in 1892, but it later became a beloved holiday tradition worldwide.

6. Ballerinas wear tutus, a short, layered skirt, for classical ballet performances. The traditional Romantic tutu is longer, reaching mid-calf, while the classical tutu is shorter and stiffer.

7. Pyotr Ilyich Tchaikovsky is regarded as one of the greatest ballet composers. His works, including Swan Lake, The Nutcracker, and Sleeping Beauty, are still widely performed today.

8. The role of the male dancer evolved over time. In the 19th century, male dancers were considered mere supports for the ballerinas, but today they showcase athleticism and technical prowess.

9. Ballet dancers often suffer from injuries due to the demanding nature of the art form. Common injuries include sprained ankles, stress fractures, and tendonitis.

"Spinning like a graceful tornado!"

10. The iconic ballet move, the pirouette, involves spinning on one leg while maintaining balance and control. Dancers can execute multiple pirouettes in quick succession, showcasing their skill.

11. The first full-length ballet, La Sylphide, was choreographed by Filippo Taglioni in 1832 and introduced the concept of ethereal, otherworldly female characters.

"The ultimate toe challenge!"

12. The ballet technique "en pointe" requires years of training and strength. It involves dancing on the tips of the toes, supported by pointe shoes.

13. Ballet performances are often accompanied by live orchestras, with the music and dance seamlessly intertwining to create a harmonious experience for the audience.

Classical Literature

1. Beowulf, the Old English epic poem, is one of the oldest surviving works of literature in the English language, dating back to the 8th century.

2. The Roman poet Virgil's epic poem "The Aeneid" was commissioned by Emperor Augustus as a literary work to legitimize his rule and connect Rome's founding to the Trojan War.

3. The Greek playwright Sophocles won the Athenian dramatic competition 24 times, surpassing his contemporaries Aeschylus and Euripides in popularity and skill.

4. The Ancient Greek playwright Aristophanes was known for his comedies, including "Lysistrata," which depicted women's power and activism.

"Empowering women since ancient Greece!"

Art and Literature

5. The Roman poet Horace's Ars Poetica, written in the 1st century BCE, is considered one of the earliest treatises on literary criticism and offers advice to aspiring poets.

6. The Divine Comedy by Dante Alighieri is an allegorical journey through Hell, Purgatory, and Heaven, and is considered a masterpiece of Italian literature.

"Love poems lost in translation!"

7. The Greek poet Sappho, known as the "Tenth Muse," wrote lyrical poetry that explored themes of love and desire, but much of her work has been lost over time.

8. The Roman poet Catullus's passionate and sometimes explicit love poems addressed to his lover Lesbia have influenced love poetry for centuries.

9. The Epic of Gilgamesh, an ancient Mesopotamian epic poem, predates classical literature and is considered one of the earliest surviving works of literature.

10. The Roman poet Lucretius's philosophical poem "De Rerum Natura" explores Epicurean philosophy and the nature of the universe, atoms, and human existence.

11. The Roman playwright Plautus wrote popular comedies, often featuring stock characters and humorous situations, influencing later playwrights like Shakespeare.

"Rome's ultimate roast master!"

12. The Roman poet Martial's epigrams were short, witty poems that often satirized Roman society and prominent figures of his time.

13. The tragic playwright Aeschylus, known as the "Father of Tragedy," introduced the concept of a second actor on stage, expanding the possibilities of dramatic storytelling.

14. The Greek poet Pindar composed victory odes to honor athletes who won in the ancient Olympic Games, celebrating their achievements and immortalizing their glory.

Famous Authors

1. Fyodor Dostoevsky, the Russian literary giant, narrowly escaped execution for his involvement in a banned intellectual group before becoming a renowned author.

   "The disappearing mystery queen!"

2. Agatha Christie, the Queen of Crime, disappeared for 11 days in 1926, leaving the world puzzled. She was found later, claiming amnesia.

3. Charles Dickens had a pet raven named Grip, who inspired characters in his works and even received a mention in "Barnaby Rudge."

4. Mark Twain, known for his humor, was born during the appearance of Halley's Comet in 1835 and predicted he would die during its next return in 1910. He was right.

5. J.R.R. Tolkien, the creator of Middle-earth, was also a talented

Art and Literature

illustrator and drew intricate maps and illustrations for his stories.

6. Jane Austen initially wrote her novels anonymously and only received recognition as the author after her death.

"The ultimate survivor's tale!"

7. Ernest Hemingway survived multiple brushes with death, including shrapnel wounds, plane crashes, and two consecutive plane crashes in Africa.

8. Louisa May Alcott, author of "Little Women," worked as a nurse during the American Civil War and contracted typhoid fever as a result.

9. Leo Tolstoy, famous for "War and Peace," was once excommunicated from the Russian Orthodox Church for his controversial beliefs.

10. Roald Dahl, the beloved author of children's books, was a World War II fighter pilot and a spy for British intelligence.

"A pen name for protection!"

11. George Orwell, known for his dystopian novel "1984," adopted his pen name to protect his family's reputation while writing controversial political essays.

12. Harper Lee, the author of "To Kill a Mockingbird," was childhood friends with Truman Capote and assisted him in his research for "In Cold Blood."

13. Oscar Wilde, known for his wit, was imprisoned for "gross indecency" due to his homosexuality and wrote his famous poem "The Ballad of Reading Gaol" during his incarceration.

14. Arthur Conan Doyle, the creator of Sherlock Holmes, believed in spiritualism and even became friends with illusionist Harry Houdini, who debunked many spiritualist claims.

Famous Paintings

1. Leonardo da Vinci's famous painting "Mona Lisa" is known for her enigmatic smile, but did you know the reason behind her fame is still debated?

2. Vincent van Gogh's masterpiece "Starry Night" depicts a view from his asylum room window and includes a hidden image of the planet Venus.

3. The Scream by Edvard Munch is an iconic painting that captures existential dread. Surprisingly, Munch created four versions of it, including two in pastel.

    "Melted cheese, melted minds!"

4. Salvador Dalí's surrealist masterpiece, "The Persistence of Memory," with its melting clocks, was inspired by a piece of Camembert cheese melting under the sun.

5. Claude Monet's "Water Lilies" series consists of around 250

paintings, all inspired by his beautiful garden in Giverny, France.

6. The intricate details in Hieronymus Bosch's triptych painting "The Garden of Earthly Delights" contain bizarre and fantastical creatures, sparking endless interpretations.

7. Grant Wood's iconic painting "American Gothic" features a farmer and his daughter, but they were actually the artist's sister and their dentist, not a husband and wife.

8. The focal point of Johannes Vermeer's "The Art of Painting" is a map of the Netherlands, highlighting the importance of Dutch art during the Golden Age.

"Abstractly Expensive!"

9. Jackson Pollock's abstract expressionist painting "No. 5, 1948" is one of the world's most expensive artworks, with a record sale price of over $140 million.

10. Leonardo da Vinci's "The Last Supper" was originally painted with experimental materials, causing the paint to deteriorate, and subsequent restorations have altered the original appearance.

11. The Birth of Adam by Michelangelo, found on the Sistine Chapel ceiling, depicts the moment God breathes life into Adam, a powerful representation of creation.

12. Les Demoiselles d'Avignon by Pablo Picasso, considered a groundbreaking piece of early 20th-century art, was initially met with shock and confusion due to its radical departure from traditional forms.

"Twice the pain, twice the talent!"

13. In Frida Kahlo's self-portrait "The Two Fridas," she depicts herself twice, symbolizing her dual Mexican and European heritage and her emotional and physical pain.

Explorers and Expeditions

1. While searching for the Northwest Passage, Sir John Franklin's lost expedition mysteriously vanished in 1845, leading to numerous rescue attempts and the discovery of the fabled passage years later.

2. Explorer Jacques Cartier encountered a strange sight during his voyage in 1534 when he discovered an island inhabited by what he thought were women, but were actually indigenous men who wore furs.

3. Robert Falcon Scott's ill-fated Terra Nova Expedition in 1912 aimed to be the first to reach the South Pole, but tragically, he and his team perished on the return journey just 11 miles away from a vital supply depot.

   "Epic voyages, underrated fame!"

4. The legendary Chinese admiral Zheng He led seven epic

History and Exploration

expeditions in the early 15th century, sailing vast treasure fleets that reached as far as Africa, but his achievements were largely forgotten in later years.

5. In 1911, Hiram Bingham discovered the ancient Inca city of Machu Picchu high in the Andes Mountains of Peru, but initially, he believed it to be Vilcabamba, the lost city of the Incas.

6. Norwegian explorer Roald Amundsen, who beat Robert Scott to the South Pole, also ventured into the skies as the first person to fly over the North Pole in an airship in 1926.

"South America's original data nerd!"

7. In the early 19th century, Alexander von Humboldt conducted an ambitious scientific expedition across South America, collecting extensive data and producing groundbreaking research that influenced many fields of study.

8. Polar explorer Ernest Shackleton's Endurance expedition encountered disaster when their ship became trapped in Antarctic ice in 1915, but remarkably, all crew members survived after an extraordinary journey of resilience.

9. The Viking explorer Leif Erikson is believed to have reached North America around the year 1000, nearly 500 years before Christopher Columbus, and established a settlement in what is now Newfoundland, Canada.

"America's original road trip!"

10. The Lewis and Clark expedition, commissioned by President Thomas Jefferson in 1804, aimed to explore the newly acquired western territory of the United States, reaching the Pacific Ocean.

11. The Apollo 11 mission, led by Neil Armstrong, Buzz Aldrin, and Michael Collins, successfully landed the first humans on the moon on July 20, 1969, marking a monumental achievement in space exploration.

Famous Architects

1. Frank Lloyd Wright, the legendary American architect, designed over 1,000 structures during his career, including the iconic Fallingwater and the Guggenheim Museum in New York City.

   "Breaking barriers, one prize at a time!"

2. Zaha Hadid, an Iraqi-British architect, was the first woman to receive the Pritzker Architecture Prize, often referred to as the Nobel Prize of Architecture.

3. Maya Lin, an American architect and artist, gained fame for her design of the Vietnam Veterans Memorial in Washington, D.C., which she created while still a college student.

4. Renzo Piano, the Italian architect behind the Shard in London and the Centre Pompidou in Paris, has a passion for playing the piano and often incorporates musical themes in

History and Exploration

his designs.

"Architect by day, pianist by night!"

5. Ludwig Mies van der Rohe, a German-American architect, popularized the phrase "less is more" and is known for his minimalist approach and sleek designs, such as the Barcelona Pavilion.

6. Eileen Gray, an Irish architect and furniture designer, created innovative and functional pieces, including the iconic adjustable "E.1027" table, now considered a design classic.

7. Jeanne Gang, an American architect, gained recognition for her innovative approach to sustainable design, such as the Aqua Tower in Chicago, featuring undulating balconies.

8. Shigeru Ban, a Japanese architect, is known for his humanitarian work, using recyclable materials to create temporary structures for disaster-stricken areas around the world.

"Skyscrapers have never been the same!"

9. Louis Sullivan, considered the "father of skyscrapers," coined the phrase "form follows function," emphasizing the importance of designing buildings based on their intended use and purpose.

10. Denise Scott Brown, an American architect, played a crucial role alongside her husband, Robert Venturi, in shaping postmodern architecture and challenging architectural conventions.

11. Moshe Safdie, an Israeli-Canadian architect, designed Habitat 67 in Montreal, an innovative housing complex featuring stacked and interconnected modular units.

12. Kazuyo Sejima, a Japanese architect, co-founded the firm SANAA and is recognized for her minimalist designs, characterized by clean lines and the extensive use of glass.

Famous Astronomers

1. Henrietta Swan Leavitt, an astronomer who worked at Harvard, discovered the period-luminosity relationship in Cepheid variable stars, which led to the measurement of cosmic distances.

2. Nicolaus Copernicus, famous for his heliocentric model, also studied medicine, law, and economics, and even served as a church administrator.

3. Vera Rubin, an astronomer known for her groundbreaking work on dark matter, overcame gender barriers to become the first female astronomer allowed to observe at Palomar Observatory.

   "From sci-fi dreams to cosmic realities!"

4. Carl Sagan, renowned for popularizing science, was also a science fiction writer and co-wrote the screenplay for the

History and Exploration

movie "Contact."

"When stars go on a diet!"

5. Subrahmanyan Chandrasekhar, an astrophysicist, proposed the Chandrasekhar limit, which defines the maximum mass a white dwarf star can attain before collapsing into a neutron star or black hole.

6. Hypatia, an ancient astronomer from Alexandria, was the first woman to make significant contributions to the field but was tragically murdered in 415 CE.

7. Edwin Hubble, after whom the Hubble Space Telescope is named, was initially a lawyer but switched careers to become one of the most influential astronomers of the 20th century.

"Hydrogen's advocate, universe's queen!"

8. Cecilia Payne-Gaposchkin, an astronomer and astrophysicist, discovered that hydrogen is the most abundant element in the universe, despite initial resistance to her findings.

9. Clyde Tombaugh, the astronomer who discovered Pluto, also discovered several asteroids and advocated for classifying Pluto as a planet.

10. In addition to discovering Uranus, William Herschel constructed over 400 telescopes and cataloged numerous deep-sky objects during his career.

11. Annie Maunder, a British astronomer, made significant contributions to solar studies and was one of the first women to work as a science writer for a major newspaper.

12. Ejnar Hertzsprung, a Danish astronomer, independently developed the Hertzsprung-Russell diagram, a fundamental tool for classifying and understanding stars.

13. Subramanyan Chandrasekhar won the Nobel Prize in Physics in 1983 for his theoretical studies on the physical processes that occur during the later stages of stellar evolution.

Famous Battles

1. The Battle of Hastings in 1066 saw the Norman invasion of England led by William the Conqueror, resulting in the defeat of King Harold II and the Norman establishment of power.

2. The Battle of Waterloo in 1815 marked the final defeat of French emperor Napoleon Bonaparte, ending his reign and reshaping European politics.

    "Tea and Victory!"

3. The Battle of Agincourt in 1415 saw a decisive victory for the English army led by King Henry V, despite being greatly outnumbered by the French.

4. The Battle of Salamis in 480 BCE saw a Greek naval fleet under Themistocles defeat the larger Persian fleet, securing Greek independence and changing the course of history.

5. The Battle of Tours in 732 CE marked the halt of the Muslim

History and Exploration

expansion into Europe, as Frankish forces led by Charles Martel repelled an invading Muslim army.

6. The Battle of Yorktown in 1781 was the final major American Revolution battle, resulting in British forces surrendering under General Cornwallis to American and French troops.

7. The Battle of Midway in 1942 was a naval confrontation between the United States and Japan, where American forces inflicted significant damage on the Japanese navy.

8. The Battle of Tours in 451 CE saw a coalition of Roman and Visigothic forces led by Aetius defeat the Huns, preventing their advance into Gaul.

9. The Battle of Austerlitz in 1805 was a resounding victory for Napoleon, where French forces defeated a combined Austro-Russian army, leading to the dissolution of the Holy Roman Empire.

"Nelson's Navy Drops the Beat!"

10. The Battle of Trafalgar in 1805 was a naval engagement between the British Royal Navy and the French-Spanish fleet, resulting in a decisive British victory under Admiral Horatio Nelson.

11. The Battle of Guadalcanal fought from 1942 to 1943 in the Pacific Theater of World War II, marked the first major offensive by Allied forces against the Japanese Empire.

12. The Battle of Plataea in 479 BCE marked the final Greek victory over the Persians in the Greco-Persian Wars, effectively ending the Persian threat to Greek independence.

"Aetius Saves the Day!"

13. The Battle of Chalons in 451 CE saw a coalition of Roman and Visigothic forces led by Aetius defeat the combined forces of the Huns and their allies, preventing their conquest of Western Europe.

Famous Bridges

1. The Brooklyn Bridge, connecting Manhattan and Brooklyn in New York City, was the first bridge in the world to be constructed using steel wire cables.

2. The Tower Bridge in London, UK, features a glass walkway on its high-level walkways, allowing visitors to see the bridge and river beneath their feet.

   "When steel goes big!"

3. Sydney Harbour Bridge in Australia has a total length of 1,149 meters (3,770 feet) and required approximately 52,800 tons of steel to construct.

4. The Charles Bridge in Prague, Czech Republic, is adorned with 30 statues of saints, each with its own story and historical significance.

5. The Millau Viaduct in France is the tallest bridge in the world,

History and Exploration

standing at 343 meters (1,125 feet) tall, even taller than the Eiffel Tower.

6. The Akashi Kaikyo Bridge in Japan, with a span of 1,991 meters (6,532 feet), is the longest suspension bridge in the world.

7. The Forth Bridge in Scotland, UK, is a UNESCO World Heritage Site and is considered one of the greatest engineering achievements of the Victorian era.

8. The Bridge of Sighs in Venice, Italy, got its name from the sighs of prisoners who walked across it as it led them from the Doge's Palace to the prison.

"A bridge that spans two worlds!"

9. The Bosphorus Bridge in Istanbul, Turkey, is one of the few bridges in the world that spans two continents, connecting Europe and Asia.

10. The Pont du Gard in France is an ancient Roman aqueduct bridge built around the 1st century AD, and is a UNESCO World Heritage Site.

11. The Chapel Bridge in Lucerne, Switzerland, is the oldest wooden covered bridge in Europe and is decorated with beautiful 17th-century paintings.

12. The Chengyang Wind and Rain Bridge in China is made entirely of wood and features covered walkways, pavilions, and a pagoda-like structure.

"Spiraling through traffic like a boss!"

13. The Nanpu Bridge in Shanghai, China, has a spiral approach ramp that allows vehicles to ascend and descend the bridge smoothly.

14. The Vasco da Gama Bridge in Lisbon, Portugal, is the longest in Europe, stretching over 17 kilometers (10.6 miles) across the Tagus River.

Famous Buildings

"Imagine getting lost in that elevator!"

1. The Burj Khalifa in Dubai is the tallest building in the world, reaching a staggering height of 828 meters, with 163 floors.

2. The Great Wall of China, spanning over 21,000 kilometers, is not a single continuous wall but a series of fortifications built over centuries.

3. The Guggenheim Museum in Bilbao, Spain, is renowned for its unique design by Frank Gehry, resembling a giant ship or a metallic flower.

4. The Louvre Museum in Paris, France, was originally a medieval fortress before being converted into a grand museum housing masterpieces like the Mona Lisa.

5. The Potala Palace in Lhasa, Tibet, is the highest ancient palace in the world, standing at an elevation of 3,700 meters above

History and Exploration

sea level.

"That's a lot of acres to explore!"

6. The Angkor Wat temple complex in Cambodia is the largest religious monument in the world, covering an area of over 400 acres.

7. The Chichen Itza pyramid in Mexico features a remarkable acoustic phenomenon known as the "Clapping Echo," where a clap produces a unique echo.

8. The St. Basil's Cathedral in Moscow is renowned for its vibrant onion domes and was built to celebrate the capture of Kazan from Mongol forces.

"Someone forgot to polish Lady Liberty!"

9. The Statue of Liberty in New York City was a gift from France, and its copper exterior has developed a distinctive green patina over time.

10. The Neuschwanstein Castle in Germany, which inspired Disney's Sleeping Beauty Castle, was built as a personal retreat for King Ludwig II of Bavaria.

11. The Machu Picchu citadel in Peru was constructed using sophisticated engineering techniques that have allowed it to withstand earthquakes for centuries.

12. The Forbidden City in Beijing, China, served as the imperial palace for over five centuries and is home to around 9,000 rooms.

13. The Giza Pyramid Complex in Egypt includes the Great Pyramid of Giza, one of the Seven Wonders of the Ancient World and the oldest intact pyramid.

14. The Hanging Gardens of Babylon, one of the Seven Wonders of the Ancient World, were a stunning feat of engineering and horticulture, though their exact location remains a mystery.

Famous Castles

1. Edinburgh Castle in Scotland houses the oldest crown jewels in Britain, including the Stone of Destiny, which has been used in coronations since the 9th century.

2. Neuschwanstein Castle in Germany served as the inspiration for the iconic Disney castle and is an architectural masterpiece of the 19th century.

3. Himeji Castle in Japan, also known as the "White Heron Castle," survived centuries without being damaged by earthquakes, wars, or fires.

    "Fang-tastic!"

4. Bran Castle in Romania, often associated with Dracula, was never actually inhabited by the famous vampire but was a residence of medieval Hungarian kings.

5. Château de Chambord in France boasts an extraordinary

History and Exploration

"Avoiding awkward encounters since 1519!"

double-helix staircase designed by Leonardo da Vinci, allowing two people to ascend and descend without meeting.

6. Windsor Castle in England is the oldest and largest inhabited castle in the world, serving as a royal residence for over 900 years.

7. Prague Castle in the Czech Republic is listed in the Guinness World Records as the largest ancient castle complex, covering an area of over 70,000 square meters.

8. Edinburgh Castle's Great Hall in Scotland is believed to be haunted by the ghost of a piper who vanished while exploring the tunnels beneath the castle.

"Where jewels and Beefeaters hang out!"

9. The Tower of London in England has housed the Crown Jewels since the 14th century and is protected by the iconic Yeomen Warders, also known as Beefeaters.

10. Chillon Castle in Switzerland inspired Lord Byron's famous poem "The Prisoner of Chillon" and features a mysterious subterranean labyrinth.

11. The Alhambra in Spain, a UNESCO World Heritage site, showcases exquisite Islamic architecture and breathtaking gardens with intricate water features.

12. Edinburgh Castle's One o' Clock Gun tradition began in 1861, where a cannon fires a shot precisely at 1 p.m. every day except Sundays.

13. The Mont Saint-Michel Abbey in France is an architectural marvel perched on a rocky island and is only accessible during low tide via a causeway.

14. The Tower of London served as a menagerie for exotic animals, including a polar bear that was allowed to swim and catch fish in the River Thames.

Great Leaders in History

1. Julius Caesar, the Roman leader, was said to suffer from seizures, possibly indicating that he had epilepsy.

2. Nelson Mandela, the renowned South African leader, studied law in secret while he was imprisoned on Robben Island.

   "Impressive, Mandela!"

3. Mahatma Gandhi, the Indian independence activist, was nominated for the Nobel Peace Prize five times but never won.

4. Queen Elizabeth I of England spoke multiple languages fluently, including Latin, French, Spanish, and Italian.

5. Joan of Arc, the French military leader, claimed to have been visited by saints and heard divine voices guiding her during battles.

6. Abraham Lincoln, the 16th President of the United States, was

History and Exploration

"From president to plant whisperer!"

a licensed bartender and owned a tavern in Illinois.

7. George Washington, the first President of the United States, was an avid horticulturist and experimented with different plant varieties.

8. Cleopatra, the last active pharaoh of Egypt, was known for her linguistic abilities and could speak at least seven languages.

9. Martin Luther King Jr., the civil rights leader, skipped two grades in high school and entered college at the age of 15.

10. Alexander the Great, the Macedonian king, named over 70 cities after himself, including Alexandria in Egypt.

11. Genghis Khan, the Mongol conqueror, promoted religious freedom and practiced a policy of tolerance towards different faiths.

12. Queen Victoria of the United Kingdom proposed to her husband, Prince Albert, rather than the other way around.

"President turned Amazonian adventurer!"

13. Theodore Roosevelt, the 26th President of the United States, was an adventurer and explored the Amazon rainforest.

14. Indira Gandhi, India's first female Prime Minister, led her country during a state of emergency from 1975 to 1977.

Greek Mythology

"The original overprotective husband!"

1. Zeus, the king of the gods, once swallowed his first wife, Metis, to prevent her from giving birth to a child more powerful than him.

2. Pandora, the first woman on Earth, was not only responsible for releasing all evils into the world but also held hope inside her jar.

3. The Sirens, seductive sea creatures with enchanting voices, were actually half-bird and half-woman hybrids.

4. In Greek mythology, Hades, the ruler of the Underworld, was not considered evil but rather maintained a sense of justice in the afterlife.

5. The winged horse Pegasus, born from the blood of Medusa, was tamed by the hero Bellerophon, who rode him into many

History and Exploration

epic battles.

"The ultimate bad hair day!"

6. Medusa, known for her snake-like hair and deadly gaze, was originally a beautiful mortal woman until she was cursed by the goddess Athena.

"Causing love troubles since ancient times!"

7. Eros, the god of love, is often depicted as a young, mischievous boy with wings and a bow and arrow to inspire passion in mortals.

8. The Furies, also known as the Erinyes, were vengeful goddesses who pursued and punished those guilty of crimes such as murder and perjury.

9. Orpheus, a gifted musician, ventured into the Underworld to rescue his beloved wife, Eurydice, but tragically lost her on his way back.

10. Hephaestus, the god of fire and craftsmanship, was born with a physical deformity and was later married to the beautiful goddess Aphrodite.

11. Persephone, the daughter of Demeter, was abducted by Hades and became the Queen of the Underworld, spending part of the year there.

12. The Trojan War, described in Homer's Iliad, was sparked by a golden apple inscribed with the words "to the fairest" and led to the fall of Troy.

13. The goddess Athena, known for her wisdom and strategic prowess, sprang fully formed from the head of Zeus, wearing armor and a helmet.

14. Cerberus, the three-headed dog guarding the gates of the Underworld, prevented the living from entering and the dead from escaping.

Historic Events

1. During the American Revolutionary War, British soldiers enjoyed playing a game called "rounders," which later evolved into baseball.

2. The Great Fire of London in 1666 was inadvertently started by a small flame in a bakery on Pudding Lane.

3. The Titanic's sister ship, the Britannic, was repurposed as a hospital ship during World War I before sinking in the Aegean Sea.

4. The D-Day invasion during World War II required an extensive amount of rubber, prompting a massive collection of used condoms for recycling.

   "Rubber, the unsung hero of D-Day!"

5. The Boston Tea Party, a pivotal event in the American Revolution, was executed by a group of colonists disguised as

History and Exploration

Mohawk Indians.

6. The eruption of Mount Vesuvius in 79 AD preserved the Roman city of Pompeii, giving us invaluable insight into ancient daily life.

"Waterloo, where Napoleon finally met his match!"

7. The Great Wall of China took centuries to build and was constructed using a mixture of rice flour, lime, and sticky rice.

8. The Battle of Waterloo, a decisive moment in European history, was fought in present-day Belgium and marked Napoleon Bonaparte's final defeat.

9. The Chernobyl disaster in 1986 released an amount of radiation 400 times greater than the atomic bomb dropped on Hiroshima.

"One giant leap for waste management systems!"

10. The Apollo 11 mission, which landed humans on the moon for the first time, carried a total of 96 bags of urine and feces back to Earth.

11. The opening ceremony of the first modern Olympic Games in 1896 included a speech in ancient Greek and the release of 300 pigeons.

12. The Berlin Wall, a symbol of the Cold War, was constructed overnight in 1961 and stood for almost three decades.

13. The Hindenburg disaster in 1937, where the German airship burst into flames, was recorded by radio reporter Herbert Morrison, whose emotional commentary became famous.

14. The eruption of Mount Tambora in 1815 caused the "Year Without a Summer" in 1816, leading to crop failures and widespread hunger around the world.

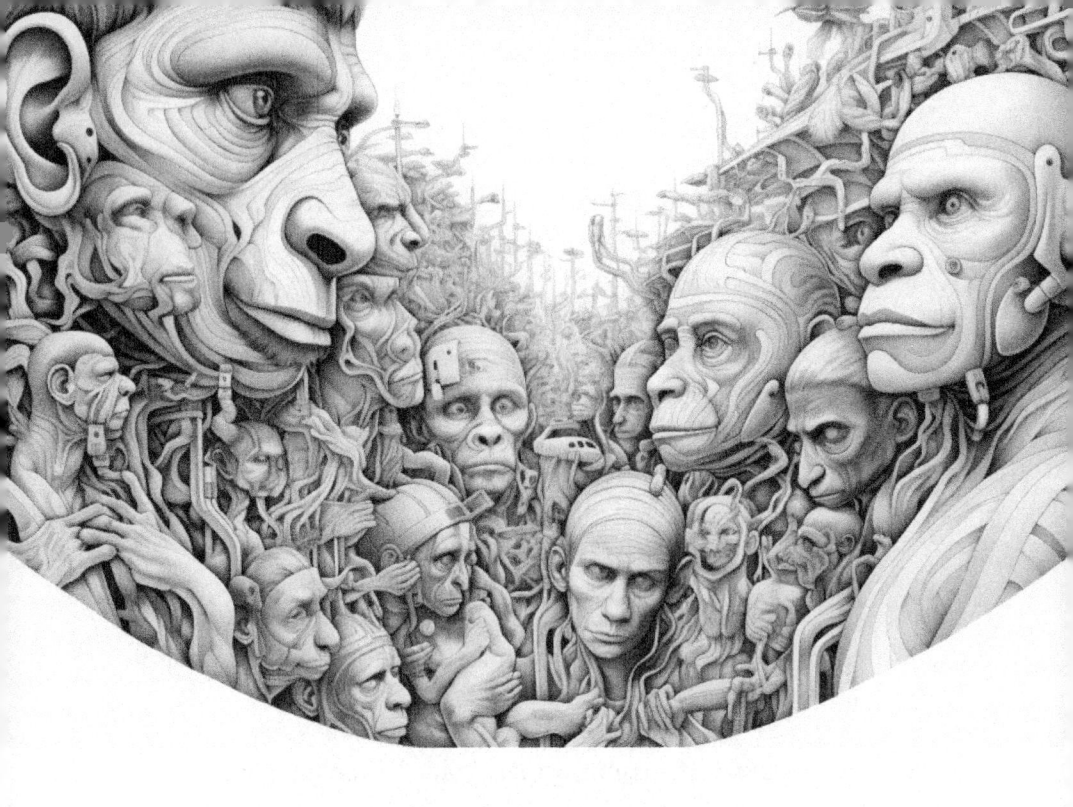

Human Evolution

1. The oldest known hominid fossil, Sahelanthropus tchadensis, dates back approximately 7 million years, providing insights into early human evolution.

2. Homo naledi, a recently discovered species, shares both primitive and advanced features, suggesting complex evolutionary relationships within our family tree.

3. Genetic studies reveal that modern humans possess trace amounts of Neanderthal and Denisovan DNA, indicating interbreeding between these species.

4. The expansion of Homo sapiens out of Africa around 70,000 years ago led to the eventual colonization of the entire world.

   "World conquerors since 70,000 years ago!"

5. The emergence of bipedalism, or walking on two legs, is a significant milestone in human evolution, providing

Anatomy

        advantages for survival and resource acquisition.

6. Homo habilis, often referred to as the "handy man," was one of the earliest species to create stone tools, highlighting technological advancements in our lineage.

7. Mitochondrial Eve is a theoretical ancestor who lived in Africa around 200,000 years ago and is the most recent common matrilineal ancestor of all living humans.

"The ultimate family tree mess!"

8. Human evolution is not a linear progression but rather a complex, branching pattern with multiple species coexisting at different times.

9. The study of ancient DNA has revealed the existence of other hominin groups, such as the mysterious "Ghost population" known as the Denisovans.

10. Humans share a common ancestry with other primates, such as chimpanzees and bonobos, with whom we diverged around 6-8 million years ago.

11. The discovery of Homo naledi fossils in a deep and isolated chamber suggests that early humans may have intentionally disposed of their dead.

"Language, our superpower of chit-chat!"

12. The ability to speak and communicate through language is a unique trait of humans, contributing to our social complexity and cultural development.

13. The evolution of our teeth and jaws has been influenced by changes in diet, reflecting adaptations to different food sources throughout our history.

14. The ongoing field of paleogenomics allows scientists to extract and analyze ancient DNA, unraveling the intricate details of human evolutionary history.

Human Psychology

1. Choice overload refers to the negative consequences of having too many options, as it can lead to decision paralysis and decreased satisfaction with the chosen option.

    "I've seen this fact so many times, I love it!"

2. The "mere-exposure effect" suggests that people tend to develop a preference for things they are repeatedly exposed to, even if they are initially neutral or unfamiliar.

3. Implicit bias refers to unconscious attitudes or stereotypes that affect our judgments and behavior, often without our awareness.

4. The "bystander effect" reveals that individuals are less likely to offer help in an emergency situation when others are present, assuming someone else will take action.

5. Serial position effect states that people tend to recall

information from the beginning and end of a list more easily than items in the middle.

6. Halo effect is the tendency to form an overall positive impression of a person based on one positive trait or characteristic.

7. Cognitive dissonance theory suggests that people have a motivational drive to reduce the discomfort caused by inconsistencies between their beliefs and actions.

"Forget the rest, remember the first!"

8. The "primacy effect" demonstrates that people are more likely to remember information presented at the beginning of a list or sequence. The Zeigarnik effect reveals that unfinished or interrupted tasks tend to be better remembered than completed ones.

9. The overjustification effect occurs when providing extrinsic rewards for intrinsically motivated activities leads to a decrease in intrinsic motivation.

10. The spotlight theory of attention proposes that attention is like a spotlight, focusing on specific aspects of the environment while ignoring others.

"I heard it before, it must be true!"

11. The illusory truth effect suggests that people are more likely to believe information that they have heard before, even if it is false.

12. The mere ownership effect shows that people tend to place a higher value on objects they own, simply because they own them.

13. The framing effect demonstrates that people's choices can be influenced by how options are presented or "framed," even if the underlying information remains the same.

The Human Body

1. The human brain generates about 25 watts of power while awake, enough to power a light bulb.

2. The average person produces enough saliva in their lifetime to fill two swimming pools.

   "The ultimate razor blade dissolver!"

3. The acid in your stomach is strong enough to dissolve razor blades.

4. If all the blood vessels in your body were laid end to end, they would stretch around the Earth over 4 times.

5. The human eye can distinguish up to 10 million different colors.

6. Your nose can remember about 50,000 different scents.

Anatomy

7. The strongest muscle in the human body is the masseter, which allows you to chew with incredible force.

"Blood squirting champion!"

8. The human heart can create enough pressure to squirt blood up to 30 feet if a blood vessel is severed.

9. The surface area of your lungs is roughly the size of a tennis court.

10. Your skin is the largest organ in your body, weighing about 8 pounds and covering an area of about 22 square feet.

11. The human body has more bacteria cells than human cells, with trillions of bacteria living in and on us.

12. Your bones are composed of a matrix that is stronger than steel, although they are more lightweight.

"Humans 1, sharks 0, even in the afterlife!"

13. Human teeth are just as strong as shark teeth and can even outlast the rest of the body after death.

14. The human body has enough iron to make a 3-inch nail, enough carbon to make 900 pencils, and enough fat to make seven bars of soap.

15. The average person will produce enough saliva in their lifetime to fill two bathtubs.

16. The length of all the nerves in your body combined could stretch over 600 miles.

17. Your tongue is covered in small bumps called papillae, which contain taste buds that help you detect flavors.

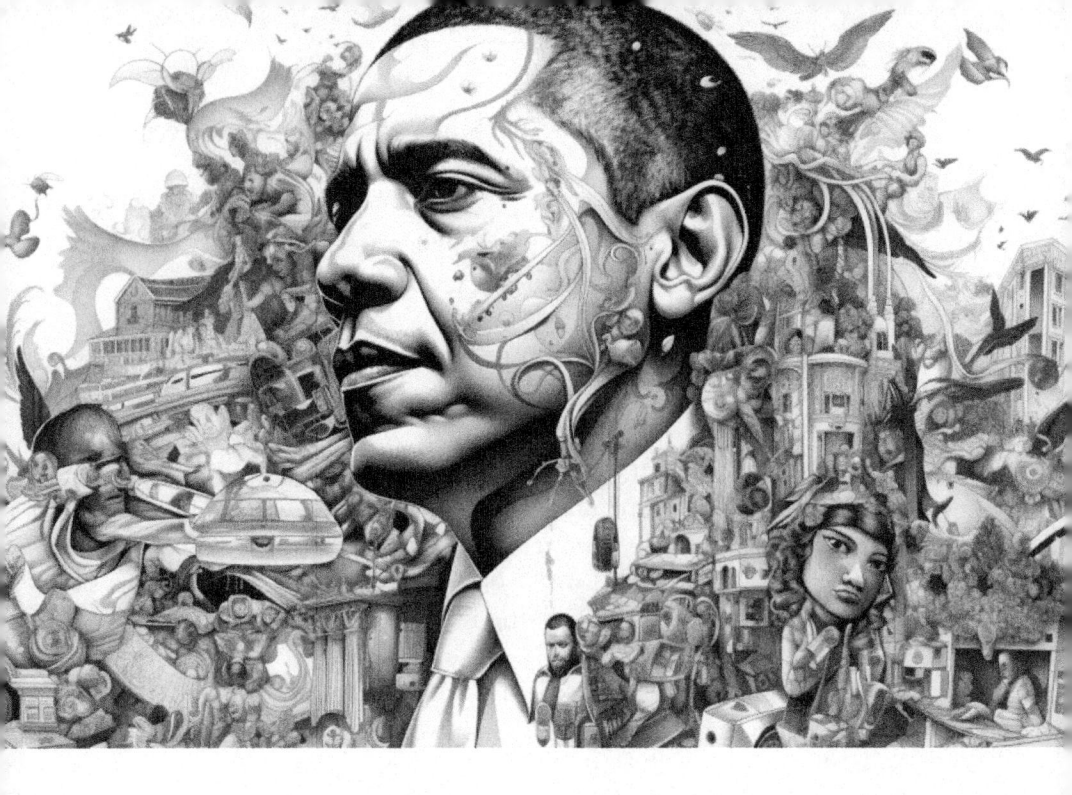

Barack Obama

1. Barack Obama's full name is Barack Hussein Obama II. His middle name, Hussein, is of Swahili origin and means "good" or "handsome."

2. Prior to becoming the 44th President of the United States, Obama served as a senator from Illinois, making him the fifth African American senator in U.S. history.

   "Bringing aloha vibes!"

3. He is the first U.S. president to have been born in Hawaii, making him the only president not born in the contiguous United States.

4. As a child, Obama was given the nickname "Barry" by his family, and it wasn't until college that he started using his given name, Barack.

5. Obama is multilingual and can speak English, Indonesian, and

some Spanish. He learned Indonesian during his childhood years when he lived in Jakarta.

"Ballin' leader!"

6. Obama is a big fan of basketball and played the sport throughout his life. He even installed a basketball court in the White House during his presidency.

7. In his younger days, Obama experimented with various recreational drugs, including marijuana and cocaine, which he candidly admitted in his memoir.

8. Despite being the president, Obama never forgot his love for comics and was a big fan of Spider-Man when he was growing up.

9. During his time in the White House, Obama became the first sitting president to publish a scientific paper, which focused on his cancer research initiative.

"Related to Brad Pitt!"

10. He is a distant relative of Brad Pitt. They share a common ancestor, Edwin Hickman, who lived in Virginia in the 1760s.

11. Obama has a unique way of dealing with stress – he enjoys chewing Nicorette gum, which he began using to quit smoking before his presidential campaign.

12. His favorite book is "Moby-Dick" by Herman Melville. He has stated that he rereads it frequently to remind himself of the epic struggle between man and nature.

13. He has a strong connection to Ireland through his ancestors. A small village in County Offaly, Ireland, named Moneygall, proudly claims him as a distant relative.

14. He is left-handed, making him the seventh left-handed president in U.S. history. Other notable left-handed presidents include Bill Clinton and George H.W. Bush.

Bill Gates

1. Bill Gates co-authored a computer program called Traf-O-Data at age 17 to analyze traffic patterns, his first venture.

    "800/800 in math, nailed it!"

2. He scored 800 out of 800 in the math section of the SAT, demonstrating his early aptitude for problem-solving.

3. Gates reads approximately 50 books per year and maintains a blog where he shares book reviews.

4. He is a certified helicopter pilot and often flies around in his private helicopter.

5. To predict and prevent disease outbreaks, Gates invested $100 million in pandemic preparedness research.

6. Bill Gates owns a rare collection of Leonardo da Vinci's original writings and sketches.

People

7. He joined the giving pledge, promising to donate most of his wealth to philanthropy during his lifetime.

8. Gates became a knight in the Order of the British Empire in 2005.

"Harvard's loss, Microsoft's gain!"

9. Gates dropped out of Harvard University in his sophomore year to co-found Microsoft with Paul Allen.

10. Gates wrote a popular book, "The Road Ahead," which was published in 1995.

11. Gates was fascinated by early computers and wrote his first computer program at age 13.

"Fear of flying, but still soaring!"

12. He has a fear of flying and used to avoid it until he realized it was hindering his work.

13. In high school, he was part of a group of programmers who were banned from using the computer for some time due to hacking.

14. Gates purchased the Codex Leicester, a collection of Leonardo da Vinci's scientific writings, for over $30 million.

15. Despite being one of the world's richest people, he washes dishes every night to relax.

16. Gates was once arrested in New Mexico for a traffic violation, and he had to post bail.

17. In his younger days, he was a talented and competitive bridge player.

18. He has received honorary doctorates from several universities worldwide.

19. Bill Gates regrets not being able to speak multiple languages fluently.

Donald Trump

1. Donald Trump's uncle, John G. Trump, was an MIT professor who examined Nikola Tesla's papers after his death.

2. Trump was the fourth U.S. President to face impeachment, with the House voting to impeach him in 2019 and 2021.

3. He once owned the New Jersey Generals, a team in the United States Football League, during the 1980s.

4. Trump is a teetotaler and does not drink alcohol, citing the death of his older brother due to alcoholism. *"Cheers to sobriety!"*

5. In 1990, he was honored with a star on the Hollywood Walk of Fame for his contributions to television.

6. Donald Trump has filed for corporate bankruptcy six times, mostly related to his casino and hotel businesses.

People

7. He appeared in cameos in several films and television shows, including "Home Alone 2" and "The Fresh Prince of Bel-Air."

8. Trump once launched a board game called "Trump: The Game" in 1989, but it was a commercial failure.

9. In 1999, he proposed running for President as a third-party candidate with the Reform Party but later abandoned the idea.

10. Trump's family name was originally "Drumpf" before it was changed several generations ago.

11. He is the first U.S. President to have been married three times.

"No handshakes... shake on it?"

12. Trump has a fear of germs and prefers to avoid shaking hands, especially during his presidency.

13. He is an avid user of Twitter and had one of the most followed accounts before being permanently suspended.

"Apprentice to POTUS!"

14. Donald Trump is the first President to have hosted a reality TV show, "The Apprentice."

15. He is known for his elaborate hairstyle, and he once revealed that he spends time styling it himself.

16. Trump owns golf courses around the world, and he reportedly spends a lot of time playing golf.

17. He was once involved in a lawsuit with comedian Bill Maher over a bet related to Barack Obama's birth certificate.

18. Trump's childhood nickname was "Donnie," and he attended the New York Military Academy during his teenage years.

19. He received a star on the WWE Hall of Fame in 2013 for his appearances in wrestling events.

Elon Musk

"From South Africa to Mars!"

1. Elon Musk was born in South Africa in 1971 and moved to Canada at age 17, before becoming a U.S. citizen.

2. Musk founded Zip2, an online city guide, which was acquired for $307 million in 1999.

3. PayPal, co-founded by Musk, revolutionized online payments and was later sold to eBay for $1.5 billion.

4. Musk was the inspiration for Tony Stark's character in the "Iron Man" movies.

5. He founded SpaceX in 2002 with the goal of reducing space travel costs and colonizing Mars.

6. Musk faced financial struggles and had to borrow money to keep his companies afloat in the early 2000s.

7. The idea for Tesla Motors came to Musk during a conversation about electric cars in 2004.

8. Musk is known for his hands-on approach, often sleeping on the factory floor during Tesla's production challenges.

9. He once made a bet on Twitter to build a giant battery in South Australia within 100 days, and he delivered.

10. Musk's "Hyperloop" concept aims to revolutionize transportation with high-speed pods in low-pressure tubes.

11. He has expressed concern about the dangers of artificial intelligence and has called for regulation.

12. Musk launched the Boring Company to develop tunneling technology for urban transportation.

13. He revealed plans for Neuralink, a company focused on merging the human brain with artificial intelligence.

14. Musk played a significant role in creating OpenAI, an organization promoting friendly AI development.

15. In 2020, Musk became the world's richest person briefly, surpassing Jeff Bezos.

16. He has been involved in ventures like SolarCity and OpenAI to promote renewable energy and AI safety.

"A name like no other!"

17. Musk named his son "X Æ A-12," though he later clarified the name as "X Ash Archangel."

"Flamethrowers for sale!"

18. He once sold flamethrowers through The Boring Company, garnering both attention and criticism.

19. Musk's vision for SpaceX includes a city on Mars with a million residents by the end of the century.

Greta Thunberg

1. Greta Thunberg was born on January 3, 2003, in Stockholm, Sweden, and rose to prominence as a climate activist at just 15 years old.

2. She first gained attention by striking alone outside the Swedish Parliament in 2018, sparking the global "Fridays for Future" climate strike movement.

3. Greta has Asperger's syndrome, which she considers a superpower, helping her stay focused and determined in her activism. *"Asperger's rocks!"*

4. Greta's family has a history of environmental activism, with her mother, Malena Ernman, being an opera singer and her father, Svante Thunberg, an actor.

5. She is a vegetarian and has encouraged people to adopt a

plant-based diet to reduce their carbon footprint.

6. As of 2021, she had more than 10 million followers across social media platforms, amplifying her climate message globally.

"Youngest 'Person of the Year' ever!"

7. Time magazine named her the "Person of the Year" in 2019, making her the youngest recipient of this prestigious honor.

8. Despite her fame, Greta strives to lead a simple life, avoiding flying due to its environmental impact and preferring trains and other sustainable modes of transport.

9. She declined several environmental awards, explaining that she wanted the focus to be on climate action, not individual recognition.

10. In 2020, Greta co-authored a collection of her speeches titled "No One Is Too Small to Make a Difference."

11. She donated the prize money from these speeches to environmental organizations working on climate solutions.

12. Greta's influence on young people worldwide has led to school strikes for climate, with students demanding governments prioritize sustainability.

13. She has addressed numerous world leaders and organizations, including the United Nations, European Parliament, and the World Economic Forum.

"Young climate warriors rise!"

14. Greta's climate activism has inspired the "Greta Thunberg Effect," where young activists around the world have followed her lead.

15. She has been nominated for the Nobel Peace Prize multiple times, reflecting the global recognition of her dedication to climate advocacy.

Kim Jong-un

"Time traveler, perhaps?"

1. Kim Jong-un was born on January 8, 1983 (exact date disputed). His mother is Ko Yong-hui, a dancer, and his father was Kim Jong-il.

2. He became the Supreme Leader of North Korea after his father's death in December 2011, despite having limited experience and being very young at the time.

3. The title "Supreme Leader" and "Dear Respected" are used to describe Kim Jong-un in North Korea's state media, emphasizing his authority and status.

4. Kim Jong-un has promoted a policy called "Byungjin," which aims to develop both the country's nuclear weapons program and its economy in tandem.

5. Kim Jong-un's elder half-brother, Kim Jong-nam, fell out of

People

"Living life on the dangerous side!"

favor with their father and lived mostly in exile, before being assassinated in 2017.

6. Despite leading a regime known for human rights abuses, he has shown a fascination with pop culture, and even allowed the performance of Disney characters in North Korea.

7. Kim Jong-un has purged and executed several high-ranking officials during his rule, consolidating power and eliminating potential threats to his regime.

8. Kim Jong-un's distinctive hairstyle has become somewhat of a trend in North Korea, where men are encouraged to emulate their leader's look.

9. He married Ri Sol-ju in 2009, and she is the first North Korean First Lady to be publicly acknowledged since the rule of his grandfather, Kim Il-sung.

"The ultimate hide-and-seek champion!"

10. He is known for his reclusive lifestyle and maintaining strict control over information and media within North Korea, resulting in limited exposure to the outside world.

11. His birthday is designated as a public holiday in North Korea called "Day of the Shining Star," celebrating his birth and the Kim family's leadership.

12. Kim Jong-un has met with several international leaders, including former U.S. President Donald Trump, to discuss issues related to denuclearization and diplomacy.

13. His official biography in North Korea attributes miraculous events to his birth, claiming he could walk at three weeks old and drive a car by age three.

14. He is the youngest head of state in the world, leading one of the most secretive and isolated countries.

Mark Zuckerberg

1. He turned down offers from major tech companies before finally dropping out of college to focus on Facebook.

2. Zuckerberg once had a rule to wear a gray T-shirt every day to simplify his wardrobe decisions.

3. He is color-blind, which partly influenced Facebook's blue color scheme due to its visibility to him.

4. Mark's net worth has fluctuated dramatically, and at one point, he was the youngest self-made billionaire globally.

   "Baby billionaire!"

5. His first coding project was a messaging program called "ZuckNet," built for his family at the age of 12.

6. In 2010, he pledged to donate half of his wealth to charity through the "Giving Pledge" initiative.

People

"Beefing up his principles!"

7. He became a vegetarian in 2011, and his personal challenge for the year was to only eat meat from animals he had killed.

8. Zuckerberg studied Mandarin and held Q&A sessions in Chinese during visits to China, impressing many.

9. He built an AI-powered home automation system, voiced by Morgan Freeman, named "Jarvis" in 2016.

10. Mark and his wife, Priscilla Chan, pledged to donate 99% of their Facebook shares to philanthropic efforts.

11. He has faced controversies, including privacy issues and accusations of not doing enough to combat fake news.

12. Zuckerberg appeared before Congress in 2018 to testify on Facebook's data privacy and security practices.

13. His love for Ancient Rome led him to learn Latin, and he named his second daughter "August" after Emperor Augustus.

14. Mark set himself a goal of reading a book every two weeks and shares his reading list with his Facebook followers.

15. In 2015, he and Priscilla Chan launched the Chan Zuckerberg Initiative to focus on global challenges like education and health.

16. Zuckerberg started coding at a young age, writing games on his Atari computer as a child.

"$1 billion, and the ghost of regret!"

17. He once offered $1 billion to Snapchat's founders to buy the company, but they declined the offer.

18. Despite his massive success, Mark Zuckerberg maintains a relatively simple lifestyle and remains a private person in many ways.

Meghan Markle

1. Meghan Markle was born on August 4, 1981, in Los Angeles, making her the first American to marry into the British royal family.

   "From calligraphy to royalty!"

2. Before her acting career, Meghan worked as a freelance calligrapher, which showcased her artistic skills and attention to detail.

3. Besides her acting career, Meghan is an advocate for women's rights, working as a UN Women's Advocate and promoting gender equality.

4. She has a love for calligraphy and even used her skills to handwrite wedding invitations for celebrities like Paula Patton.

5. She is known for her love of rescue dogs and adopted two pups, Guy and Bogart, before moving to the UK.

People

6. Meghan and Prince Harry met on a blind date arranged by a mutual friend in London, and they kept their relationship private initially.

"Real-life royal drama!"

7. She appeared in several TV shows and movies, with a notable role as Rachel Zane in the legal drama series "Suits."

8. The couple got engaged in November 2017, with Prince Harry proposing during a cozy night at home while roasting a chicken.

9. Meghan's engagement ring contains two diamonds from Princess Diana's personal collection, making it even more meaningful.

"Soup kitchen royalty!"

10. Meghan is a self-proclaimed foodie and enjoys cooking, which led her to volunteer at a soup kitchen in LA.

11. Meghan's wedding to Prince Harry on May 19, 2018, was a historic event as it embraced diversity and inclusivity.

12. Her wedding veil was adorned with floral representations of all 53 Commonwealth countries, symbolizing unity and global cooperation.

13. She has a strong love for handwritten letters and often sends personalized notes to friends and supporters.

14. Meghan is a vocal advocate for mental health awareness, openly discussing her struggles with anxiety and seeking therapy.

15. Despite the royal title, Meghan faced harsh media scrutiny, leading her and Prince Harry to step back from their senior royal roles.

16. Alongside Prince Harry, she founded Archewell, an organization focusing on charitable endeavors, audio content, and other impactful projects.

Pope Francis

1. Pope Francis was born Jorge Mario Bergoglio in Argentina, the first Pope from the Americas and the Southern Hemisphere.

2. Before becoming Pope, he worked as a nightclub bouncer and a chemical technician.

   "From nightclub bouncer to Pope!"

3. He is the first Jesuit Pope and the first Pope to take the name Francis, inspired by St. Francis of Assisi.

4. Pope Francis has a love for tango dancing and used to dance with his then-girlfriend at parties.

5. He has only one functioning lung due to an infection in his youth, which hasn't hindered his active lifestyle.

6. Pope Francis is known for his humble lifestyle, choosing to live in a simple Vatican guesthouse instead of the papal

apartments.

7. He often performs spontaneous acts of kindness, such as inviting homeless individuals to dine with him.

8. He's the first Pope to have an active social media presence, with millions of followers on Twitter and Instagram.

"Prayers in many tongues!"

9. He is fluent in Spanish, Italian, and German, besides his native language of Spanish.

10. Pope Francis is a huge fan of soccer, supporting the Argentine club San Lorenzo and even has a club membership.

11. He used to take public transportation and was known to have used a regular bus while he was the Archbishop of Buenos Aires.

12. Pope Francis has a deep concern for refugees and migrants and has advocated for their rights and dignity.

13. He has written a book called "Sobre el Cielo y la Tierra" ("On Heaven and Earth") with a rabbi, showcasing interfaith dialogue.

14. Pope Francis once worked as a janitor in a lab during his studies at a technical school.

15. He chose to be consecrated as a bishop on the feast of St. George, his father's name day.

16. Pope Francis is the first Pope to have a background in chemistry.

"Justice, equality, and love!"

17. Pope Francis has been outspoken on issues like income inequality, poverty, and social justice, urging world leaders to address these challenges.

Prince Harry

1. Prince Harry's full name is Henry Charles Albert David, and he was born on September 15, 1984, in London, England.

2. He is the younger son of Prince Charles and Princess Diana, and his official title is His Royal Highness Prince Henry of Wales.

   "From war zone to red carpet!"

3. Prince Harry is the first British royal to have served on active duty in a war zone since his uncle, Prince Andrew, during the Falklands War.

4. Prince Harry served in the British Army, completing two tours of duty in Afghanistan, rising to the rank of Captain.

5. Known for his philanthropic work, Harry co-founded Sentebale, a charity supporting children affected by HIV/AIDS in Lesotho.

People

6. Harry is a passionate advocate for mental health awareness and co-founded the mental health initiative Heads Together with his brother William and sister-in-law Kate.

7. Prince Harry and Meghan stepped back from their senior royal roles in 2020 and moved to California with their son, Archie.

8. He and Meghan signed a deal with Netflix to produce documentaries, docu-series, feature films, and children's shows.

9. Harry co-authored a memoir scheduled for release in 2022, promising to share the "definitive account" of his life experiences.

10. He has traveled extensively, representing the British monarchy and engaging with various communities worldwide.

11. Harry is a skilled pilot and has flown Apache attack helicopters during his military service.

"A royal stage star!"

12. As a child, he had a passion for performing arts and participated in school plays.

13. In 2013, Harry and a group of injured British servicemen reached the South Pole to raise funds for charity.

14. He has faced controversies in the media but has also been praised for his openness about mental health struggles.

15. Prince Harry is a conservation advocate and supports numerous environmental initiatives.

"Royalty, but approachable!"

16. Despite being part of the royal family, he is known for his down-to-earth personality and approachability.

17. He is known for his playful and sometimes humorous interactions with the public, making him a beloved figure worldwide.

Queen Elizabeth II

1. During World War II, young Princess Elizabeth joined the Women's Auxiliary Territorial Service and trained as a mechanic and military truck driver.

2. She and Prince Philip are distant cousins; they share a great-great-grandmother, Queen Victoria, making them third cousins.

3. Queen Elizabeth II owned all the swans in England, an ancient tradition dating back to the 12th century known as the "Swan Upping."

4. She has sent over 50,000 congratulatory messages to centenarians in the United Kingdom during her reign.

"50,000 congratulations!"

5. Queen Elizabeth II spoke fluent French, a skill she demonstrated during state visits and meetings with French dignitaries.

People

6. Her Majesty has met every U.S. president since Harry S. Truman, except Lyndon B. Johnson, who declined her invitation to visit.

7. She broke tradition by allowing her 1947 wedding to Prince Philip to be broadcast on the radio for the public to hear.

"The Queen's royal convenience!"

8. Queen Elizabeth II had her own private ATM at Buckingham Palace, installed in 1986 by Coutts Bank.

9. Her official birthday was celebrated on a Saturday in June, known as the "Trooping the Colour" parade.

"Dorgis rule!"

10. The Queen had a unique breed of dogs known as "dorgis," a cross between corgis and dachshunds.

11. The Queen had a talent for mimicking voices and often entertained her family with her impersonations.

12. Her wardrobe featured vibrant colors and bold prints to ensure she remained visible in large crowds.

13. The Queen's official birthday was different from her actual birth date; she was born on April 21, 1926.

14. Queen Elizabeth II sent her first email in 1976 during a visit to an army base.

15. She received over 3.5 million items of correspondence during her reign.

16. The Queen had a special relationship with her Prime Ministers and met with them privately each week when she was in London.

17. Queen Elizabeth II was the first British monarch to visit Australia and New Zealand in 1954 and has made numerous visits to both countries since.

Vladimir Putin

1. Vladimir Putin was a judo champion during his youth, earning a black belt and later becoming the honorary president of the International Judo Federation.

   "KGB secret agent turned judo master!"

2. He worked as a KGB officer in East Germany during the Cold War, where he adopted the alias "Mikhailov" to keep his identity secret.

3. In 2007, Time magazine named him the "Person of the Year," recognizing his significant global influence and political prowess.

4. Despite his strong image, Putin has shown his emotional side by shedding tears in public on a few occasions, especially when discussing national tragedies.

5. Putin is fluent in several languages, including German, English,

"Fluent in languages and politics!"

and French, which has aided his diplomacy and international interactions.

6. He is known for his adventurous side, having participated in activities like piloting fighter jets and diving in submarines.

7. Putin is a fan of Russian literature and has cited Leo Tolstoy's "War and Peace" and Fyodor Dostoevsky's works as some of his favorites.

8. He has a judo move named after him called the "putin," which is a tricky counterattack technique used in the sport.

9. Putin has been involved in numerous publicized stunts, such as flying with migrating cranes to guide them on their journey and tranquilizing a tiger in the wild.

10. Putin has held several high-ranking political positions in Russia, including serving as Prime Minister before becoming President.

"Puck playing Putin in action!"

11. He is an avid hockey player and often participates in exhibition games with former NHL players and Russian hockey stars.

12. Putin's early career involved working as a spy in the KGB's foreign intelligence division, where he developed valuable espionage skills.

13. He was once photographed holding a pistol and tranquilizing darts while visiting a research center for Siberian tigers.

14. Putin has been portrayed in various forms of media, from cartoons to action figures, highlighting his global recognition and controversial image.

15. He was involved in the 1999 operation to suppress Chechen separatist forces, earning him both praise and criticism for his tough stance.

Famous Scientists

"Physics and Potions: Newton's secret life!"

1. Sir Isaac Newton, known for his laws of motion, was obsessed with alchemy and spent more time studying it than physics.

2. Marie Curie's notebooks are still radioactive due to her extensive work with radioactive materials, and they are stored in lead-lined boxes.

3. Galileo Galilei was the first person to discover that the Milky Way is made up of countless individual stars, challenging the prevailing belief that it was a single nebula.

4. Charles Darwin suffered from a mysterious illness for most of his life, causing various symptoms such as fatigue, headaches, and heart palpitations.

5. Isaac Newton, one of history's greatest scientists, was also an avid inventor, developing designs for windmills and even a

Science

mechanical calculator.

"Einstein: the sockless genius!"

6. Albert Einstein never wore socks and would often go barefoot, claiming it made him feel more connected to the Earth.

7. Leonardo da Vinci, known for his artistic masterpieces, was also a brilliant scientist and inventor who conceptualized flying machines, tanks, and diving suits.

8. Marie Curie was the first woman to win a Nobel Prize and the only person to have won Nobel Prizes in two different scientific fields (Physics and Chemistry).

9. Nikola Tesla claimed to have received signals from outer space and believed he had made contact with intelligent beings from other planets.

10. Thomas Edison, the inventor of the phonograph and the modern electric light bulb, was largely self-taught and had only three months of formal education.

11. Stephen Hawking, renowned theoretical physicist, made significant contributions to the understanding of black holes while battling the debilitating motor neuron disease, ALS.

"The ultimate genius autopsy!"

12. Albert Einstein's brain was preserved after his death, and it has been studied extensively to try to understand the physical basis for his genius.

13. Charles Darwin's voyage on the HMS Beagle, where he collected specimens and made observations, greatly influenced his groundbreaking theory of evolution.

14. Rosalind Franklin's contributions to the discovery of DNA's structure were initially overlooked, and she received little recognition until after her death.

Genetics and DNA

1. DNA, the blueprint of life, can store incredible amounts of information. One gram of DNA can hold over 215 petabytes, equivalent to 215 million gigabytes of data.

   "99.9% match, we're almost clones!"

2. Humans share about 99.9% of their DNA with each other. The remaining 0.1% accounts for the genetic variations that make each individual unique.

3. DNA can repair itself. Our cells have sophisticated repair mechanisms that fix damages to the DNA molecule, helping to maintain genetic integrity.

4. Genetic mutations are not always harmful. Some mutations can provide advantages, such as increased resistance to certain diseases or enhanced cognitive abilities.

5. Identical twins may have slight genetic differences. Mutations

"DNA's wrinkle-inducing alarm clock!"

can occur during embryonic development, resulting in genetic variations between twins who were once genetically identical.

6. DNA can act as a timekeeper. By examining telomeres—the protective caps at the ends of chromosomes—scientists can estimate a person's biological age and predict potential health risks.

7. Some animals have extraordinary DNA repair capabilities. For example, the tiny water bear (tardigrade) can survive extreme conditions, including exposure to radiation, by repairing its damaged DNA.

"From snail's pace to warp speed!"

8. DNA sequencing has become remarkably fast and affordable. The first human genome sequencing, completed in 2003, took over a decade and cost billions of dollars. Today, it can be done in a matter of days at a fraction of the cost.

9. DNA can be used for long-term data storage. Scientists have successfully encoded books, music, and even Shakespeare's sonnets into synthetic DNA, offering a potential solution for preserving information for centuries.

10. Some organisms have the ability to undergo horizontal gene transfer, where genes can be transferred between different species, leading to genetic diversity and evolution.

11. Genetic testing can provide insights into ancestry. By analyzing specific DNA markers, scientists can determine an individual's genetic heritage and trace their ancestral origins.

12. Some diseases are caused by alterations in mitochondrial DNA, which is inherited solely from the mother. Examples include mitochondrial disorders and Leber's hereditary optic neuropathy (LHON).

Geology and Rocks

1. The largest known crystal on Earth, found in a Mexican cave, measures a whopping 55 feet long and weighs 55 tons.

2. Geologists use a device called a petrographic microscope to analyze thin slices of rocks and minerals at a microscopic level.

3. Rocks can be classified into three main types: igneous (formed from solidified magma or lava), sedimentary (formed from sediments), and metamorphic (formed from other rocks).

"Volcanic Lego for giants!"

4. The rock formation known as the Giant's Causeway in Northern Ireland consists of around 40,000 interlocking basalt columns, created by ancient volcanic activity.

5. The Great Barrier Reef, stretching over 1,400 miles, is the largest structure on Earth created by living organisms and is primarily composed of coral, which is a rock-like substance.

Science

6. The process of plate tectonics, where Earth's lithosphere is divided into several plates that move and interact, is responsible for the formation of mountains, earthquakes, and volcanic activity.

7. Diamonds are formed deep within the Earth's mantle under extreme pressure and high temperatures, and they are brought to the surface during volcanic eruptions.

"Nature's epic rock show!"

8. The Grand Canyon in the United States is an awe-inspiring example of how rivers can carve through layers of rocks, exposing millions of years of geological history.

9. The world's largest underground cave system, the Mammoth Cave in Kentucky, USA, stretches over 400 miles and is still being explored by geologists and speleologists.

10. The Earth's magnetic field, generated by its molten iron core, acts as a protective shield against harmful solar radiation, guiding compass needles and aiding navigation.

11. The term "geode" comes from the Greek word "geoides," which means "earthlike," reflecting the rounded shape of these rock cavities resembling the Earth's shape.

"Earth's deepest belly button!"

12. The Mariana Trench, located in the western Pacific Ocean, is the deepest known point on Earth, reaching a depth of approximately 36,000 feet.

13. The term "geology" was coined by Scottish physician and naturalist James Hutton in the late 18th century, combining the Greek words for "Earth" and "study."

14. The oldest known rocks on Earth, found in Western Greenland, are estimated to be around 3.8 billion years old, providing evidence of the planet's ancient history.

Festivals and Celebrations

1. The Songkran Water Festival in Thailand, known for its massive water fights, marks the Thai New Year and symbolizes cleansing and renewal.

2. La Tomatina in Spain is a unique festival where participants engage in a massive tomato fight, using over 100,000 kilograms of tomatoes.

   "Tomatoes, the secret weapon of fun!"

3. The Boryeong Mud Festival in South Korea draws millions of visitors each year who enjoy mud-based activities, including mud slides and wrestling matches.

4. The Albuquerque International Balloon Fiesta in New Mexico, USA, is the world's largest hot air balloon festival, attracting hundreds of colorful balloons each year.

5. The Lantern Festival in Taiwan concludes the Lunar New Year

Human Society and Culture

celebrations with thousands of paper lanterns released into the night sky, creating a breathtaking spectacle.

6. The Rio Carnival in Brazil is one of the most famous festivals globally, featuring extravagant parades, samba dancing, and stunning costumes.

7. The Harbin Ice and Snow Festival in China showcases massive ice sculptures and structures, creating a stunning winter wonderland.

8. The Day of the Dead, or Dia de los Muertos, is a Mexican holiday where families honor and remember their deceased loved ones with vibrant celebrations and colorful altars.

"A daring sprint for life!"

9. The Running of the Bulls, part of the San Fermin Festival in Pamplona, Spain, sees thrill-seekers sprinting alongside charging bulls through the city's streets.

10. The Up Helly Aa festival in Lerwick, Scotland, involves a spectacular procession of Vikings, culminating in the burning of a replica Viking longship.

11. The Cherry Blossom Festival in Japan celebrates spring's arrival and cherry blossoms blooming with picnics, performances, and stunning displays.

"Let the good times roll!"

12. The Mardi Gras festival in New Orleans, USA, is famous for its lively parades, jazz music, and delicious food and drink indulgence.

13. The Pushkar Camel Fair in Rajasthan, India, brings together thousands of camels, livestock traders, and tourists for a vibrant market, competitions, and cultural events.

14. The Inti Raymi festival in Peru is a grand celebration of the Inca Empire's sun god, Inti, with colorful processions, music, and reenactments of ancient rituals.

Food and Nutrition

1. The world's oldest known recipe is a Sumerian beer recipe from around 1800 BCE, showcasing humanity's early fascination with fermented beverages.

2. Turmeric, a popular spice, contains curcumin, which has powerful anti-inflammatory properties and may help alleviate symptoms of arthritis.

3. Chocolate was once used as currency by the Mayans and Aztecs. They considered it valuable and even used cocoa beans as a form of money.

4. Spinach is not as iron-rich as once believed. A misplaced decimal point in a 19th-century study led to spinach being portrayed as an extraordinary source of iron. *"Popeye, look away!"*

5. Quinoa is technically a seed, not a grain, and it contains all

Human Society and Culture

nine essential amino acids, making it a complete protein source.

6. Pineapple is the only known source of bromelain, an enzyme that aids digestion and has anti-inflammatory properties.

"The devil's fiery creation!"

7. The highest recorded spice level on the Scoville scale is found in the Carolina Reaper, a chili pepper that can reach a mind-blowing 2.2 million Scoville Heat Units.

8. Honey never spoils. Archaeologists have discovered honey pots in ancient Egyptian tombs that are over 3,000 years old and still perfectly edible.

9. The term "superfood" has no scientific definition but is commonly used to describe nutrient-dense foods like blueberries, salmon, and kale.

10. The durian, known for its strong smell, is banned in some hotels, public transportation, and airports in Southeast Asia due to its potent odor.

"Worth its weight in... saffron!"

11. The world's most expensive spice is saffron, derived from the crocus flower. It takes about 150 flowers to produce just one gram of saffron.

12. Tomatoes were once considered poisonous in Europe due to their resemblance to toxic plants. It wasn't until the 18th century that they gained popularity as food.

13. The blue color of blueberries is caused by anthocyanins, powerful antioxidants linked to improved brain function and reduced risk of heart disease.

14. The fruit we commonly refer to as a "banana" is technically a berry, while strawberries, raspberries, and blackberries are not considered berries but "aggregate fruits."

Global Cultures

1. In Japanese culture, it is customary to present gifts using both hands as a sign of respect and gratitude.

2. The Maasai people of East Africa greet each other by spitting on their hands before shaking hands, symbolizing trust and goodwill.

3. In India, the Namaste gesture, with palms pressed together and a slight bow, is a common way to greet others and show respect.

"Iceland rocks!"

4. In Iceland, there is a belief in hidden people called "Huldufólk," and many Icelanders actively avoid disturbing the rocks and hills where they are said to live.

5. The Himba tribe of Namibia considers red ochre paste an essential beauty product, applying it to their skin and hair to

Human Society and Culture

protect them from the harsh desert climate.

6. The Aymara people of the Andes have a unique way of perceiving time: they believe the past is in front of them and the future lies behind.

7. In Thailand, it is considered impolite to touch someone's head as it is believed to be the most sacred part of the body.

"Life's colorful reunion!"

8. The Day of the Dead, celebrated in Mexico, is a vibrant festival where families gather to honor and remember their deceased loved ones through colorful decorations and offerings.

9. In South Korea, the number four is considered unlucky because its pronunciation is similar to the word for "death."

10. In Aboriginal culture, Dreamtime stories are passed down orally through generations, explaining the creation of the world and guiding moral values.

11. In Brazil, the dance martial art known as capoeira blends acrobatics, music, and martial arts, originally developed by enslaved Africans as a form of self-defense.

12. The Thai tradition of Loy Krathong involves releasing beautifully crafted floating baskets made of banana leaves onto rivers and lakes to pay respect to the water goddess.

"Breaking plates, not friendships!"

13. In Greece, breaking plates during celebrations, known as "sirtaki," is a tradition believed to bring good luck and ward off evil spirits.

14. The Holi festival in India is a riot of colors where people throw vibrant powdered pigments at each other, symbolizing the arrival of spring and the victory of good over evil.

Human Rights

1. The Universal Declaration of Human Rights, adopted by the United Nations in 1948, is the most translated document in the world, available in over 500 languages.

2. The concept of human rights dates back to ancient civilizations, with the Code of Hammurabi, created in 1754 BCE, containing some early legal protections for individuals.

3. The right to education is recognized as a fundamental human right. However, approximately 263 million children worldwide are still out of school.

4. Although not explicitly mentioned in the Universal Declaration, the right to privacy has been recognized by international bodies and courts as a fundamental human right.

   "A trilogy that everyone should read!"

5. The International Bill of Human Rights consists of three core

documents: the Universal Declaration of Human Rights, the International Covenant on Civil and Political Rights, and the International Covenant on Economic, Social, and Cultural Rights.

"Think, believe, and change your mind!"

6. The right to freedom of thought, conscience, and religion is protected under international law, allowing individuals to hold their own beliefs or change them without coercion.

7. The concept of "human security" emerged in the 1990s, recognizing that the well-being of individuals is vital for the stability and development of societies.

8. The United Nations Human Rights Council is responsible for promoting and protecting human rights globally and addressing human rights violations.

9. Freedom of expression is a fundamental human right that allows individuals to voice their opinions, ideas, and creativity without censorship or repression.

"Home, sweet home!"

10. The right to adequate housing is recognized as a basic human right, yet more than 1.6 billion people worldwide lack access to adequate housing.

11. The Convention on the Rights of the Child, adopted in 1989, is the most widely ratified human rights treaty in history, affirming children's rights worldwide.

12. The right to peaceful assembly and association allows individuals to gather, protest, and form organizations to advocate for their rights and causes.

13. The right to freedom of movement protects individuals' ability to travel, migrate, and seek asylum without arbitrary restrictions or discrimination.

Influencers

1. Influencers can earn substantial incomes through brand collaborations, with some top-tier influencers commanding fees of up to $1 million per post.

2. Surprisingly, the term "influencer" was officially added to the English Oxford Dictionary in 2019, reflecting the cultural significance of this digital phenomenon.

   "Trust me, I'm an influencer!"

3. In some cases, influencers' followers trust them more than traditional celebrities, considering them more authentic and relatable.

4. Instagram is one of the most popular platforms for influencers, with over 1 billion active users and an estimated 500,000 influencers on the platform.

5. Micro-influencers with smaller but highly engaged audiences

Human Society and Culture

are gaining traction as brands seek more targeted and genuine connections with consumers.

6. Some influencers have successfully transitioned into traditional media, landing roles in TV shows, movies, and even becoming published authors.

"Big impact in small circles!"

7. Brands are increasingly using nano-influencers, individuals with fewer than 10,000 followers, to tap into hyper-local and niche markets.

8. Influencer fraud is a growing concern, with some influencers buying fake followers or engagement to deceive brands and inflate their influence.

9. The travel industry benefits from influencers showcasing picturesque destinations, but they also face criticism for promoting overtourism and unsustainable practices.

10. Some influencers have faced legal troubles for failing to disclose sponsored content, leading to regulations and increased transparency requirements.

11. Influencers are constantly under pressure to create and share content, leading to burnout and mental health issues.

12. The influencer industry has sparked the rise of "influencer houses", where multiple influencers live together, creating collaborative content and expanding their reach.

13. Influencers often collaborate with other influencers to cross-promote content, leveraging each other's audiences for mutual growth.

"Riding the waves of online influence!"

14. The world of influencers continues to evolve as new platforms, technologies, and trends emerge, reshaping the dynamics of online influence.

Native American Cultures

1. Native American cultures are incredibly diverse, with over 500 distinct tribes with unique languages, traditions, and belief systems.

   "Moms know best!"

2. Many Native American tribes practiced matrilineal descent, where lineage and inheritance were traced through the mother's line.

3. The concept of "dream catchers" originated from the Ojibwe tribe and was traditionally used to filter out bad dreams and allow good dreams to pass through.

4. The Anasazi people of the southwestern United States built intricate cliff dwellings, such as the famous Mesa Verde, which showcased their architectural ingenuity.

5. Native Americans contributed significantly to modern

Human Society and Culture

medicine by introducing natural remedies like quinine, aspirin, and pain-relieving herbs to European settlers.

6. The Navajo Code Talkers played a crucial role in World War II, using their native language to transmit coded messages that the enemy couldn't decipher.

7. Native American artwork often incorporates intricate beadwork, quillwork, pottery, and basketry, showcasing their skilled craftsmanship and artistic traditions.

8. The Inuit people have adapted to harsh Arctic conditions and developed innovative technologies, such as the kayak and the igloo, to survive in extreme environments.

"Buffalo's number one fan club!"

9. Native American tribes like the Lakota Sioux hold the buffalo in high regard as a sacred animal that provided them with sustenance, clothing, and shelter.

10. Many Native American tribes revered the natural world, viewing animals, plants, and rivers as interconnected with their spiritual beliefs and ceremonies.

11. Native American tribes, such as the Apache and Comanche, were skilled horse riders and fierce warriors who adapted their hunting and warfare tactics with the introduction of horses by Europeans.

"The one-man writing revolution!"

12. The Cherokee syllabary, invented by Sequoyah in the early 19th century, was one of the few instances in history where a single individual created a writing system.

13. Native American cultures have rich storytelling traditions, passing down myths, legends, and oral histories through generations to preserve their heritage.

Social Media

1. The first social media platform, Six Degrees, was launched in 1997 and allowed users to create profiles and make friends online.

2. Facebook was originally limited to Harvard students and was known as "Thefacebook" when it launched in 2004.

3. Twitter was initially called "twttr" and was inspired by the idea of sending short, 140-character messages similar to SMS.

4. Instagram was developed as a location-sharing app called Burbn before it evolved into the popular photo-sharing platform we know today.

"From video dating to cat videos!"

5. YouTube, launched in 2005, was created by three former PayPal employees and was initially designed as a video dating site called "Tune In Hook Up."

Human Society and Culture

6. LinkedIn, founded in 2003, is the world's largest professional networking platform, with over 700 million users worldwide.

7. Social media platforms like Facebook and Instagram use algorithms to determine which posts users are most likely to engage with.

8. Snapchat introduced the concept of disappearing messages and Stories, revolutionizing the way people share content temporarily.

9. Mark Zuckerberg chose Facebook's blue color scheme because he is red-green colorblind, and blue is the color he sees best.

10. Pinterest, launched in 2010, was initially an invite-only platform, and users needed an invitation to join and create an account.

"Making lifetimes fly by faster!"

11. The average person spends around 2 hours and 25 minutes daily on social media, amounting to approximately 5 years and 4 months over a lifetime.

12. Social media platforms generate revenue primarily through advertising, with Facebook and Google accounting for a significant portion of online ad spending.

"The tiny symbol that ruled Twitter!"

13. The hashtag symbol (#) was popularized on Twitter as a way to categorize and search for specific topics or conversations.

14. TikTok, a short-form video platform, experienced rapid growth and became one of the most downloaded apps globally, reaching over 2 billion downloads in 2020.

Strange Country Laws

"Singapore really stuck to it!"

1. In Singapore, it is illegal to chew gum. The ban was imposed to keep the city clean and prevent gum-related litter.

2. In France, it is illegal to name a pig "Napoleon." The law aims to protect the name and legacy of the historical figure.

3. In Thailand, it is illegal to leave your house without underwear. The law promotes decency and hygiene in public spaces.

4. In Japan, it is illegal to be overweight. The government implemented the "Metabo Law" to combat obesity and promote a healthy lifestyle.

5. In Canada, it is illegal to pay with too many coins. The Currency Act restricts the number of coins you can use in a single transaction.

Human Society and Culture

6. In Australia, it is illegal to wear hot pink pants after midday on Sundays. This obscure law is part of a regional dress code.

"Danish nappy checks!"

7. In Denmark, it is illegal to start your car without first checking for children sleeping underneath it. The law prioritizes child safety.

8. In Switzerland, it is illegal to flush the toilet after 10 p.m. in apartment buildings. The rule is to maintain peace and quiet for residents.

9. In Russia, it is illegal to drive dirty cars. Motorists can be fined for operating vehicles that are visibly dirty or muddy.

10. In Italy, it is illegal to die without a proper burial plot. The law ensures the proper management of burial spaces.

11. In Brazil, it is illegal to sell or distribute Kinder Surprise eggs due to the toy inside being considered a choking hazard.

12. In Finland, it is illegal to own a TV without paying a television license fee. The fee funds public broadcasting services in the country.

13. In China, it is illegal to reincarnate without the government's permission. The law was introduced to regulate Tibetan Buddhism and control the reincarnation process.

"Fuel up or face the consequences!"

14. In Germany, it is illegal to run out of fuel on the Autobahn. Motorists are required to ensure they have enough fuel to complete their journey.

Women's Rights

1. The world's first women's rights convention was held in Seneca Falls, New York, in 1848, where the Declaration of Sentiments was adopted, demanding women's equality.

2. Women in New Zealand became the first in the world to gain the right to vote in national elections in 1893.

3. The United Nations adopted the Convention on the Elimination of All Forms of Discrimination against Women (CEDAW) in 1979, a landmark international treaty for women's rights.

4. In Saudi Arabia, women were granted the right to drive in 2018, ending the country's long-standing ban on female drivers.

   "Proving age is just a number!"

5. Malala Yousafzai, a Pakistani activist, became the youngest-ever Nobel Prize laureate in 2014 for her advocacy of girls'

education.

6. Women in Switzerland gained the right to vote in federal elections in 1971, after a lengthy struggle for suffrage.

7. Women's suffrage in the United States was achieved with the ratification of the 19th Amendment in 1920, granting women the right to vote.

8. The Beijing Declaration and Platform for Action was adopted at the United Nations Fourth World Conference on Women in 1995, outlining a global agenda for gender equality.

"Sweden takes a leap for working moms!"

9. The right to maternity leave was established in Sweden in 1955, making it the first country to implement such legislation.

"Girls rule, boys drool!"

10. Women in Rwanda hold the world record for the highest percentage of female representation in a national parliament, with women comprising over 60% of the seats.

11. The Women's Liberation Movement emerged in the late 1960s and early 1970s, focusing on various women's rights issues such as reproductive rights and workplace equality.

12. Women in India were granted the right to vote in 1950, following the country's independence from British rule.

13. The Convention on the Rights of the Child, adopted by the UN in 1989, includes specific provisions for the rights of girls and women under the age of 18.

14. The fight for women's rights continues today, with ongoing efforts to address issues such as gender-based violence, pay disparities, and political underrepresentation.

World Cuisines

"Plates you can eat!"

1. Ethiopian cuisine incorporates a sourdough flatbread called injera, which serves as both a plate and an edible utensil.

2. In Japan, the kaiseki tradition involves meticulously arranged, seasonal dishes that are visually stunning and meticulously prepared with precise cooking techniques.

3. India boasts an incredibly diverse culinary landscape, with each region having unique spices, flavors, and cooking techniques varying from mild and aromatic to fiery and robust.

4. South Korea's staple dish, kimchi, is not only a popular side dish but also a symbol of national identity. It is made by fermenting vegetables with a blend of spices.

5. Thai cuisine embraces a harmonious balance of flavors, combining sweet, spicy, sour, and savory elements to create

Human Society and Culture

"300 ways to saucy bliss!"

dishes like Tom Yum soup and Pad Thai.

6. Italian cuisine's world-renowned pasta comes in over 300 shapes and sizes, each designed to complement different sauces and ingredients.

7. Turkish cuisine features a wide variety of mezes (appetizers) that range from stuffed grape leaves to yogurt-based dips like tzatziki, offering a vibrant array of flavors.

8. Moroccan cuisine combines aromatic spices, such as cumin, cinnamon, and saffron, with fruits, nuts, and slow-cooked meats to create dishes like tagine and couscous.

9. Ethiopian coffee ceremonies are an integral part of their culture, involving the roasting, grinding, and brewing of coffee beans, which are then served in small, handle-less cups.

"Grilling meat, Argentine-style!"

10. In Argentina, the traditional meat cooking method is asado, which involves grilling large cuts of beef over an open flame, resulting in tender and juicy steaks.

11. Lebanese cuisine features a wide range of mezzes and dishes made from fresh ingredients like olive oil, lemon juice, garlic, and herbs, creating vibrant and zesty flavors.

12. Chinese hot pot is a communal dining experience where a simmering pot of flavored broth is used to cook various ingredients like meats, vegetables, and noodles.

13. Indonesian cuisine showcases a blend of flavors influenced by Indian, Chinese, and Dutch cooking, resulting in dishes like nasi goreng and rendang.

14. In Australia, bush tucker refers to traditional Aboriginal food, including kangaroo, emu, witchetty grubs, and bush tomatoes, which have sustained Indigenous communities for centuries.

World Languages

1. The endangered language Damin, spoken by the Lardil people of Australia, could only be spoken by initiated men and had a limited vocabulary of about 400 words.

2. The Basque language, spoken in the Basque Country of Spain and France, is unrelated to any other language in the world, making it a language isolate.

3. The click languages of Southern Africa, like !Xóõ, feature a variety of clicking sounds made with different parts of the tongue.

4. The oldest written language is Sumerian, which dates back to around 3200 BCE and was used in ancient Mesopotamia.

5. Mandarin Chinese is the most spoken language in the world, with over a billion native speakers.

"Mandarin, the billion-speaker club!"

Human Society and Culture

6. The Arabic alphabet is written from right to left, and its letters change shape depending on their position within a word.

7. The indigenous language Pirahã, spoken by a small tribe in the Amazon rainforest, lacks number words and uses a complex whistling system for communication.

8. The Korean writing system, known as Hangul, was developed by King Sejong the Great in the 15th century and is highly phonetic and easy to learn.

"A Babel of 800+ tongues!"

9. The island of Papua New Guinea is home to over 800 languages, making it the most linguistically diverse country in the world.

10. In the Malayo-Polynesian language family, Tagalog, spoken in the Philippines, is known for its complex system of verb affixes indicating tense, aspect, and mood.

11. The indigenous Australian languages, such as Warlpiri, often use a system of orientation, indicating the cardinal directions, as an essential part of their grammar.

12. In Japan, there are three writing systems: hiragana, katakana, and kanji, each with different purposes and levels of complexity.

13. The International Phonetic Alphabet (IPA) is a system of symbols representing the sounds of human speech, allowing linguists to transcribe any language phonetically.

"Try pronouncing that!"

14. The Welsh language, known as Cymraeg, has the longest place name in Europe: Llanfairpllgwyngyllgogerychwyrndrobwllllantysiliogogogoch.

World Religions

1. The ancient religion of Zoroastrianism, which originated in Persia, introduced the concept of heaven, hell, and the final judgment.

2. In Shintoism, the indigenous religion of Japan, it is believed that natural objects like rocks and trees possess spirits.

   "Sweeping the ground to dodge bugs!"

3. Jainism, an ancient Indian religion, teaches non-violence to such an extreme that some Jains sweep the ground in front of them to avoid stepping on insects.

4. Sikhism, founded in the 15th century, promotes equality and believes in the concept of "langar," a community kitchen where free meals are served to all.

5. The Bahá'í Faith, established in the 19th century, emphasizes the unity of all religions and believes in progressive revelation,

Human Society and Culture

where God's message evolves over time.

6. In Buddhism, the Bodhi Tree under which Siddhartha Gautama attained enlightenment is believed to be a direct descendant of the original tree.

"Going with the flow, yin and yang-o!"

7. Taoism, an ancient Chinese religion, promotes living in harmony with nature and emphasizes the concept of yin and yang.

"When marijuana meets spiritual illumination!"

8. Rastafari, a religious movement that originated in Jamaica, considers marijuana a sacrament and often incorporates it into religious rituals.

9. The Druze religion, an offshoot of Islam, originated in the 11th century and is centered around the teachings of Caliph Al-Hakim.

10. The Native American religion of Animism believes that all elements of nature, including animals and plants, possess spiritual significance.

11. The Mormon religion, also known as The Church of Jesus Christ of Latter-day Saints, believes in additional scriptures, including the Book of Mormon.

12. The African diaspora religion of Vodou, practiced primarily in Haiti, combines elements of West African spirituality and Roman Catholicism.

13. Confucianism, a Chinese ethical and philosophical system, emphasizes the importance of social harmony, filial piety, and respect for authority.

14. The religion of Scientology, founded by L. Ron Hubbard, focuses on personal development through a process called "auditing" and believes in past lives.

Sports Around the World

1. The world's oldest known sport is wrestling, dating back over 15,000 years and depicted in ancient cave paintings.

2. The sport of Sepak Takraw, popular in Southeast Asia, combines elements of soccer and volleyball using only the feet.

3. In Australia, a unique sport called "Quidditch" is played, inspired by the fictional sport depicted in the Harry Potter series.

4. The first ever recorded marathon race took place in ancient Greece, covering a distance of approximately 26.2 miles.

5. Underwater hockey, or "Octopush," requires players to use small sticks to move a puck across the bottom of a swimming pool.

"The ultimate underwater showdown!"

Sports and Entertainment

6. The game of Kabaddi originated in India and is played by two teams, with one player trying to tag members of the opposing team without taking a breath.

7. Hurling, an Irish sport, is one of the fastest field games in the world, with players using a wooden stick called a hurley to hit a small ball.

8. Calcio Storico, played in Florence, Italy, is a mix of soccer, rugby, and wrestling, with matches often turning into intense brawls.

"A race that really carries its weight!"

9. Finland hosts the World Wife Carrying Championship, where male competitors race while carrying their female partners on their backs.

10. Chess boxing combines the mental challenge of chess with the physical demands of boxing, alternating between rounds of each.

11. Shin-kicking is a traditional English sport where opponents aim to kick each other's shins until one competitor can no longer stand.

12. The small Pacific island of Nauru is renowned for its dominance in weightlifting, producing some of the world's strongest athletes per capita.

13. The game of Buzkashi, popular in Afghanistan, involves horse-mounted players competing to grab and secure a goat carcass in their goal.

14. In New Zealand, "Zorbing" is a recreational sport where participants roll downhill inside a large, transparent plastic sphere.

"Taking polo to new heights... literally!"

15. Elephant polo, a variant of traditional polo, is played in Nepal, Thailand, and other countries, with players mounted on elephants instead of horses.

Sports Legends

1. Basketball legend Michael Jordan was initially cut from his high school team, but he used that setback as motivation to become one of the greatest players of all time.

   "Serena, the bee-fearing tennis champion!"

2. Tennis champion Serena Williams has a fear of bees and has been known to run off the court during matches if she spots one.

3. Football icon Pelé scored over 1,000 career goals and once caused a ceasefire in Nigeria during a civil war so people could watch him play.

4. Ice hockey star Wayne Gretzky holds 61 records in the National Hockey League, including the most goals and assists in a career.

5. Golfer Tiger Woods is a black belt in taekwondo and has

Sports and Entertainment

"Fast as lightning, fueled by nuggets!"

competed in martial arts tournaments as a child.

6. Track and field athlete Usain Bolt, known for his lightning speed, consumed roughly 1,000 Chicken McNuggets during the 2008 Beijing Olympics.

7. Gymnastics legend Simone Biles is afraid of bees and always keeps an EpiPen with her in case of an allergic reaction.

8. Footballer Cristiano Ronaldo has no tattoos on his body because he regularly donates blood, and tattoos can temporarily disqualify him from doing so.

9. Basketball great LeBron James was an All-State football player in high school and even received scholarship offers from some colleges.

10. Formula One racer Lewis Hamilton is the first and only Black driver to win a World Championship, breaking barriers in the predominantly white sport.

11. Tennis star Roger Federer has a phobia of sitting on the edge of a bed, believing it could affect his performance on the court.

12. Baseball legend Babe Ruth was once suspended from playing baseball for an entire season for violating a league rule regarding alcohol consumption.

13. Figure skater Michelle Kwan had a cameo appearance in the 2002 movie "Ice Princess," showcasing her skills off the ice.

14. Soccer icon Diego Maradona scored a goal with his hand during the 1986 World Cup quarter-finals, famously known as the "Hand of God" goal.

"Swimming on pasta power!"

15. Swimmer Michael Phelps consumes a staggering 12,000 calories per day during training, including a diet filled with pasta, pizza, and energy drinks.

Sportsmanship and Fair Play

1. The concept of sportsmanship dates back to ancient Greece, where it was considered essential in athletic competitions to honor the gods and maintain moral values.

2. Fair play is not limited to sports; it extends to all aspects of life, promoting integrity, respect, and fairness in relationships and interactions.

3. The "Olympic Ideal" of sportsmanship was first introduced by Pierre de Coubertin, the founder of the modern Olympic Games, to emphasize the importance of fair play and camaraderie among athletes.

   "And the award for being nice goes to..!"

4. In 1963, the Fair Play Trophy was established by the International Fair Play Committee to recognize athletes who demonstrate exceptional sportsmanship beyond winning or

losing.

5. Japanese football fans gained global attention during the 2014 FIFA World Cup when they stayed behind to clean up the stadium after their team's matches, showcasing the spirit of sportsmanship.

6. Fair play includes adhering to the rules, accepting decisions made by officials, and treating opponents with respect, regardless of the outcome.

7. The "Hand of God" incident in the 1986 FIFA World Cup quarterfinals saw Argentinean footballer Diego Maradona score a goal using his hand, later admitting it was a violation of fair play.

8. In cricket, the "Spirit of Cricket" is a traditional code of conduct that emphasizes fair play, respect for opponents, and the integrity of the game.

9. In 2016, New Zealand's rugby team, the All Blacks, was awarded the World Rugby Team of the Year and the World Rugby Coach of the Year for their outstanding sportsmanship and discipline.

"He knocks them down and helps them up!"

10. Muhammad Ali, one of boxing's greatest athletes, showed sportsmanship by helping his opponent, Henry Cooper, to stand up after knocking him down in their 1963 fight.

11. In 2012, during the London Olympics, distance runners Abbey D'Agostino (USA) and Nikki Hamblin (New Zealand) displayed remarkable sportsmanship after colliding mid-race. They helped each other finish and received the Pierre de Coubertin medal.

"Protecting fans, one game at a time!"

12. In 2013, FC Barcelona's Lionel Messi stopped play during a match against Mallorca when he noticed a young fan who had run onto the field. Messi escorted the boy to safety before resuming the game.

The FIFA World Cup

1. The FIFA World Cup has been held since 1930, except in 1942 and 1946, due to World War II.

2. Uruguay hosted the inaugural tournament and won it, making them the first World Cup champions.

   "Pickles, the soccer detective!"

3. The Jules Rimet Trophy, awarded to the winners until 1970, was stolen in 1966 but later found by a dog named Pickles.

4. The 1950 World Cup in Brazil saw a shocking upset when the United States defeated England 1-0 in what is known as the "Miracle on Grass."

5. The tournament's highest-scoring match occurred in 1954 when Austria beat Switzerland 7-5 in a thrilling encounter.

6. The 1966 World Cup in England introduced the use of red

Sports and Entertainment

and yellow cards for disciplinary purposes.

7. Mexico became the first country to host the World Cup twice in 1970, and it also marked the debut of the iconic official mascot, "Juanito."

8. The 1978 World Cup in Argentina featured the first-ever official tournament anthem, "El Mundial" by Ennio Morricone.

9. Italy's Paolo Rossi won the Golden Boot and Golden Ball in 1982, leading Italy to victory after initially facing a suspension due to a betting scandal.

10. The 1994 World Cup held in the United States witnessed the first-ever penalty shootout in a final, with Brazil defeating Italy.

"Iceland, the tiny nation that roared!"

11. Iceland became the smallest nation by population to qualify for the World Cup in 2018, capturing the world's attention with their remarkable performance.

12. The 2002 World Cup, co-hosted by South Korea and Japan, was the first tournament held in Asia, and Brazil secured their record fifth title.

13. Ghana's goalkeeper Richard Kingson became the first-ever goalkeeper to save two penalties in a World Cup shootout during the 2010 tournament.

14. The 2014 World Cup in Brazil had the most goals scored in a single tournament, with a total of 171 goals.

15. Germany's Miroslav Klose became the all-time leading goal scorer in World Cup history, surpassing Ronaldo's record in 2014.

"Referees get a video buddy!"

16. The 2018 World Cup in Russia saw the introduction of the Video Assistant Referee (VAR) system to assist with key decisions.

The Olympics

"Playing with fire since 1928!"

1. The Olympic flame tradition was introduced in the 1928 Amsterdam Games to symbolize purity, representing the continuity between ancient and modern Olympic Games.

2. The 2000 Sydney Olympics included a closing ceremony segment where a "giant" inflatable kangaroo hopped around the stadium.

3. The 1900 Paris Olympics featured unusual events like live pigeon shooting and an underwater swimming race held in the Seine River.

4. The 1936 Berlin Olympics saw the introduction of the torch relay, where the Olympic flame was carried by runners from Olympia, Greece, to the host city.

5. Eddie Eagan is the only athlete to have won gold medals in

Sports and Entertainment

both the Summer and Winter Olympics. He won boxing in 1920 and bobsleigh in 1932.

6. In the 1964 Tokyo Olympics, judo became the first martial art to be included as an official Olympic sport.

7. The 1972 Munich Olympics marked the first time the Games were televised in color, allowing viewers to experience the events in vibrant hues.

8. The 1980 Moscow Olympics faced a boycott by 66 nations, led by the United States, protesting the Soviet Union's invasion of Afghanistan.

9. At the 1992 Barcelona Olympics, the Lithuanian basketball team won bronze and popularized their tie-dye T-shirts, becoming a global fashion trend.

"Age is just a number for champions!"

10. The shortest Olympic gold medalist in history was 10-year-old Dimitrios Loundras from Greece, who won a team gymnastics event in 1896.

"Beijing, where steel birds nest!"

11. The 2004 Athens Olympics marked the return of the marathon to its original route, from the city of Marathon to the Olympic Stadium.

12. The 2008 Beijing Olympics used advanced technology to create the "Bird's Nest" stadium, an architectural masterpiece made of interwoven steel.

13. In the 2012 London Olympics, Saudi Arabia sent its first female athletes to compete, making it the last country to allow women to participate.

14. The 2016 Rio Olympics featured a refugee team comprising 10 athletes from four countries who competed under the Olympic flag.

The Premier League

1. The Premier League was founded in 1992, replacing the old First Division, with Arsenal winning the first title.

2. Manchester United holds the record for the most Premier League titles, with 13 championships.

   "The ultimate underdog heroes!"

3. Leicester City's triumph in the 2015-2016 season remains one of the most remarkable underdog stories in football history.

4. Ryan Giggs, the legendary Manchester United winger, holds the record for the most Premier League assists, with 162 in his career.

5. Arsenal's "Invincibles" team of the 2003-2004 season remains the only side to go unbeaten throughout an entire Premier League campaign.

Sports and Entertainment

6. Alan Shearer is the all-time leading goal scorer in the Premier League, netting 260 goals during his career.

7. The Premier League has the highest average stadium attendance of any football league worldwide.

"Getting goals before a driver's license!"

8. The youngest goal scorer in Premier League history is James Vaughan, who found the net for Everton at the age of 16 years and 271 days.

9. Sir Alex Ferguson, the former manager of Manchester United, holds the record for the most Premier League Manager of the Month awards, with 27.

10. The Premier League introduced goal-line technology in the 2013-2014 season to help determine if a goal has been scored.

11. Manchester City holds the record for the most points in a single Premier League season, amassing 100 points in the 2017-2018 campaign.

12. Didier Drogba, the Ivorian striker, has scored the most goals in London derbies, finding the net 43 times against other London clubs.

13. The Premier League has a revenue-sharing model, where a percentage of TV rights money is distributed evenly among all 20 clubs.

"A trophy fit for a weightlifter!"

14. The Premier League trophy weighs approximately 4.5 kilograms and stands at 76 centimeters tall.

15. The fastest goal in Premier League history was scored by Shane Long, who found the net for Southampton after just 7.69 seconds.

16. The Premier League has been home to some of the world's most expensive transfers, including Paul Pogba's move to Manchester United for £89 million in 2016.

The Superbowl

1. The first Super Bowl took place on January 15, 1967, and was called the "AFL-NFL World Championship Game" until it was officially renamed in 1969.

   "That wardrobe malfunction!"

2. The halftime show at Super Bowl XXXVIII in 2004, featuring Janet Jackson and Justin Timberlake, resulted in the coining of the term "wardrobe malfunction."

3. The Lombardi Trophy, awarded to the Super Bowl champions, is named after legendary coach Vince Lombardi, who led the Green Bay Packers to victory in the first two Super Bowls.

4. Super Bowl III in 1969 was the first to use Roman numerals in its official logo, a tradition that has continued ever since.

5. The Pittsburgh Steelers hold the record for the most Super Bowl victories, having won the championship title six times.

Sports and Entertainment

> "Those commercials better be worth it!"

6. Super Bowl commercials are renowned for their high costs. In 2020, a 30-second ad spot during the game cost approximately $5.6 million.

7. The longest punt in Super Bowl history was by Steve O'Neal of the New York Jets in Super Bowl III, with a 67-yard kick.

8. The shortest punt in Super Bowl history occurred in Super Bowl XXIV when Kansas City Chiefs' Louis Aguiar had a 16-yard punt.

9. Super Bowl XXIX in 1995 holds the record for the highest-scoring game, with the San Francisco 49ers defeating the San Diego Chargers 49-26.

10. The first Super Bowl to be played indoors was Super Bowl XII, held at the Louisiana Superdome in New Orleans.

11. Super Bowl XLIV in 2010 featured the first-ever onside kick to start the second half, executed by the New Orleans Saints, leading to their victory.

> "Brady, the GOAT of Super Bowls!"

12. The New England Patriots and the Denver Broncos are tied for the most Super Bowl losses by a team, with five each.

13. Super Bowl XLVII in 2013 was the first to feature brothers as head coaches of opposing teams: John Harbaugh (Baltimore Ravens) and Jim Harbaugh (San Francisco 49ers).

14. The only Super Bowl to go into overtime was Super Bowl LI in 2017, where the New England Patriots overcame a 25-point deficit to defeat the Atlanta Falcons.

15. The New England Patriots' Tom Brady holds numerous Super Bowl records, including the most touchdown passes, passing yards, and MVP awards.

Climate Change

1. Climate change is causing shifts in bird migration patterns, with some species arriving at their breeding grounds earlier due to warmer temperatures.

2. The melting of Arctic ice is releasing ancient viruses and bacteria frozen for thousands of years, raising concerns about potential disease outbreaks.

3. Rising ocean temperatures affect coral reefs, leading to coral bleaching and endangering marine biodiversity.

4. Climate change is causing increased extreme weather events, including more frequent and intense hurricanes, droughts, and heatwaves.

5. Melting permafrost in the Arctic releases methane, a potent greenhouse gas, further contributing to climate change.

"Who knew permafrost could be so gassy?"

6. The production of cement, a major construction material, is responsible for approximately 8% of global carbon dioxide emissions.

7. Climate change can disrupt the delicate balance of ecosystems by altering the timing of plant flowering and animal hibernation cycles.

"Earth's carbon dioxide vacuum!"

8. The Amazon rainforest, often called the "lungs of the Earth," absorbs an estimated 2 billion tons of carbon dioxide each year, helping to mitigate climate change.

9. Climate change is exacerbating water scarcity issues by altering rainfall patterns and increasing evaporation rates.

"Sea levels rising, real estate sinking!"

10. Rising sea levels threaten coastal cities and communities, displacing millions of people and causing significant economic damage.

11. Climate change can affect mental health, leading to increased rates of anxiety, depression, and post-traumatic stress disorder in vulnerable populations.

12. Increased carbon dioxide levels in the atmosphere can reduce the nutritional value of staple crops like rice, wheat, and corn.

13. The melting of glaciers and ice sheets contributes to global sea-level rise, but it also exposes ancient artifacts and archaeological sites that were previously hidden.

14. Climate change can impact the global economy, with estimates suggesting that it could cost the world up to 10% of its GDP by 2100 if left unchecked.

15. The changing climate is causing shifts in the geographic ranges of many species, leading to potential disruptions in ecosystems and loss of biodiversity.

Earthquakes

1. Earthquakes can occur anywhere on Earth's surface, but most happen along tectonic plate boundaries where the movement is active.

2. The largest earthquake ever recorded had a magnitude of 9.5 and occurred in Chile in 1960, releasing energy equivalent to over 1 billion atomic bombs.

   "The earthquake that set the city on fire!"

3. The 1906 San Francisco earthquake is one of the most famous in history and resulted in widespread devastation, with fires causing significant damage to the city.

4. Seismologists use the Richter scale to measure the magnitude of an earthquake, which is logarithmic, meaning a magnitude 7 earthquake is 10 times stronger than a magnitude 6.

5. Earthquakes are caused by the sudden release of accumulated

The Environment

"Earth's fiery dance party!"

strain energy in the Earth's crust, resulting from the movement of tectonic plates.

6. The Ring of Fire, a major area in the basin of the Pacific Ocean, is highly prone to earthquakes due to the convergence of several tectonic plates.

7. Earthquakes can be categorized as shallow, intermediate, or deep, depending on their focal depth within the Earth's crust.

8. Earthquakes generate different types of waves, including primary (P), secondary (S), and surface waves, which travel at varying speeds and cause different types of damage.

9. The word "seismology" comes from the Greek word "seismos," meaning earthquake, and is the study of earthquakes and the propagation of seismic waves.

"California's notorious troublemaker!"

10. The largest fault line in the United States is the San Andreas Fault in California, which is a major source of seismic activity.

11. Earthquakes can be foreshocks, mainshocks, or aftershocks. Foreshocks are smaller tremors that occur before the main event, while aftershocks follow the mainshock.

12. The deadliest earthquake in recorded history occurred in 1556 in China, resulting in an estimated 830,000 deaths.

13. The majority of earthquakes are relatively small and go unnoticed. Seismometers worldwide record thousands of earthquakes every day, but most are of low magnitude.

14. Earthquakes can induce liquefaction, a process where saturated soil temporarily loses its strength and behaves like a liquid, leading to the sinking and tilting of structures.

15. The first seismoscope, an instrument used to detect and measure earthquakes, was invented by Chinese astronomer Zhang Heng in the 2nd century AD.

Energy Sources

1. Geothermal energy, derived from the Earth's heat, can be harnessed for electricity generation and heating, reducing greenhouse gas emissions.

2. Ocean energy, including tidal, wave, and thermal gradients, possesses vast untapped potential for renewable power generation.

    "Waves of renewable fun!"

3. Bioenergy, produced from organic matter such as biomass and biofuels, can be a sustainable alternative to fossil fuels.

4. Solar power is abundant in space due to the absence of atmospheric interference, making it a viable energy source for future space missions.

5. Piezoelectricity, generated from pressure and mechanical stress, can be harvested from everyday activities like walking

to power small devices.

6. Fusion energy, still in development, holds immense promise as a clean and virtually limitless source of power.

7. Methane hydrates, found in Arctic permafrost and under the ocean, contain significant amounts of natural gas, potentially serving as a future energy source.

8. Space-based solar power systems orbiting the Earth could provide consistent and abundant energy for global consumption.

9. Salinity gradient energy, derived from the difference in salt concentration between freshwater and saltwater, can be harvested to generate electricity.

10. Thermophotovoltaics utilize thermal radiation to generate electricity, offering a new approach to capturing and converting waste heat.

"Hydrogen, the Swiss Army knife of energy!"

11. Hydrogen, considered a versatile energy carrier, can be produced through electrolysis and used in fuel cells for electricity and transportation.

12. Magnetohydrodynamics, a technology that uses the interaction of magnetic fields and conductive fluids, has the potential to revolutionize power generation.

"Rock 'n' roll engineering!"

13. Enhanced geothermal systems involve engineering methods to harness geothermal energy even in areas without naturally occurring geothermal resources.

14. Zero-point energy, a theoretical concept, suggests that there is residual energy even in a vacuum, although harnessing it remains a challenge.

Peculiar Weather Phenomena

"Clouds doing the worm, Australia style!"

1. The Morning Glory Cloud is a rare meteorological phenomenon in Australia, where long, tubular-shaped clouds roll across the sky in a mesmerizing wave-like pattern.

2. Waterspouts are tornadoes that form over water bodies. Unlike their land-based counterparts, they are usually weaker and short-lived, but can still pose a threat to ships and coastal areas.

3. St. Elmo's Fire is a luminous phenomenon that creates a blue or violet glow around pointed objects during storms. It is caused by the ionization of the air around these objects.

4. Thundersnow is a thunderstorm that occurs during a snowstorm, resulting in lightning and thunder accompanied by heavy snowfall. It is a rare and awe-inspiring event.

The Environment

5. Ball lightning is a mysterious phenomenon in which glowing, spherical objects appear during thunderstorms. Scientists are still unsure about its origins and mechanisms.

6. The Catatumbo Lightning in Venezuela holds the record for the most lightning strikes per square kilometer annually. It is a continuous display of lightning that occurs over Lake Maracaibo.

"Nature's fiery dance moves!"

7. Fire whirls, also known as fire tornadoes, are whirlwinds of fire that form during intense wildfires. They are caused by the interaction of strong winds and fire, creating a vortex of flames.

8. The Morning Glory Cloud of the Gulf of Carpentaria in Australia can reach up to 1,000 kilometers in length and travel up to 60 kilometers per hour.

9. The Nacreous Clouds, also called polar stratospheric clouds, are beautiful, colorful cloud formations that occur at high altitudes and are often observed near the poles.

10. The Brinicle, or "Icy Finger of Death," is a rare phenomenon where a tube of ice forms downward from the ocean's surface, freezing everything it touches, including marine life.

"When the sun goes green, it's magic!"

11. The Green Flash is an optical phenomenon that occurs just before sunrise or after sunset when a green spot appears on the upper rim of the sun, lasting for a few seconds.

12. Dust devils are whirlwinds that form on dry, sunny days when intense heating of the ground creates convective currents that lift dust and debris into a spinning column.

13. The Sailing Stones in Death Valley, California, are large rocks that mysteriously move across the desert floor, leaving long tracks behind them, without any apparent human or animal intervention.

Plastic Pollution

1. Over 8 million metric tons of plastic waste enter the oceans each year, posing a grave threat to marine life and ecosystems.

   "Plastic, the gift that keeps on polluting!"

2. Plastic takes hundreds of years to decompose, meaning that the majority of plastic ever produced still exists in some form.

3. Microplastics, tiny plastic particles, have infiltrated even the most remote areas, including Arctic ice and the deep sea.

4. Plastic pollution affects more than just marine creatures—land animals and birds often mistake plastic for food, leading to serious health issues.

5. Plastic debris can transport invasive species across vast distances, disrupting native ecosystems and biodiversity.

6. Plastics can leach harmful chemicals into the environment,

potentially contaminating water sources and endangering human health.

"Marine life's worst nightmare!"

7. Discarded fishing gear, known as ghost nets, entangle marine life, causing injury, suffocation, and death.

8. The production of plastic requires large amounts of fossil fuels, contributing to greenhouse gas emissions and climate change.

9. Even seemingly innocent products like clothing release microfibers when washed, adding to the growing microplastic pollution problem.

10. Plastic pollution isn't limited to the oceans—rivers and lakes also suffer from significant plastic contamination.

"Plastic's Texas-sized empire!"

11. The Great Pacific Garbage Patch, located between Hawaii and California, is twice the size of Texas and contains an estimated 1.8 trillion pieces of plastic.

12. Plastics can break down into smaller nanoplastics, which can be ingested by marine organisms and enter the food chain.

13. Plastic pollution has economic consequences, such as reduced tourism revenue in areas heavily affected by plastic debris.

14. Plastic waste can clog waterways and contribute to flooding by obstructing the flow of water.

15. Plastic packaging, which constitutes a significant portion of plastic waste, often has a very short usage lifespan before being discarded.

16. Plastics can absorb and concentrate toxic pollutants from the surrounding environment, becoming a source of long-term contamination.

Renewable Energy

1. Renewable energy sources, such as solar and wind power, don't produce harmful greenhouse gas emissions, making them a vital solution to combat climate change.

   "Solar panels making a splash!"

2. Geothermal energy harnesses the Earth's internal heat to generate power, offering a constant and reliable source of renewable energy.

3. Floating solar farms, also known as floating photovoltaic (PV) installations, are a growing trend, allowing solar panels to be placed on water bodies like reservoirs and lakes.

4. Biomass energy utilizes organic matter like crop residues, wood, and agricultural waste to produce heat, electricity, and biofuels.

5. Ocean energy, including tidal and wave power, harnesses the

The Environment

immense power of the ocean's natural movements to generate electricity.

6. Hydrogen, considered the clean fuel of the future, can be produced using renewable energy sources and used in fuel cells for clean power generation.

7. Concentrated solar power (CSP) technology uses mirrors or lenses to focus sunlight, creating heat that can be used to produce electricity.

8. Microgrids are small-scale, localized electricity grids that can operate independently or connect to the main power grid, increasing resilience and promoting renewable energy integration.

9. Renewable energy auctions, where companies bid to produce renewable power, have proven to be effective in reducing costs and driving renewable energy deployment.

"Saving money and the planet!"

10. Renewable energy technologies, such as solar panels and wind turbines, have become increasingly affordable and efficient, contributing to their widespread adoption.

11. The International Space Station (ISS) relies on solar panels to generate electricity, demonstrating the viability of renewable energy in space exploration.

12. In some countries, wind turbines are designed to mimic the movements of trees, helping to integrate them more seamlessly into the landscape.

"A match made in green heaven!"

13. Bioenergy with carbon capture and storage (BECCS) is a technique that combines bioenergy production with carbon capture, helping to reduce greenhouse gas levels in the atmosphere.

Volcanoes

1. Volcanic lightning, also known as "dirty thunderstorms," is a rare phenomenon where lightning is generated within a volcanic plume during an eruption.

   "Snowball fight canceled!"

2. The largest volcanic eruption in recorded history occurred in 1815 when Mount Tambora in Indonesia erupted, causing a global climate anomaly known as the "Year Without a Summer" in 1816.

3. Volcanic ash can be incredibly dangerous for airplanes, as it can damage aircraft engines and reduce visibility, leading to numerous flight cancellations and disruptions.

4. The term "pyroclastic flow" refers to a fast-moving, deadly mixture of hot gases, ash, and volcanic rocks that can reach speeds of over 400 km/h (250 mph).

The Environment

5. The world's largest volcanic caldera, the Toba Caldera, is in Sumatra, Indonesia. It measures approximately 100 kilometers by 30 kilometers (62 miles by 19 miles).

6. Volcanic eruptions can release enormous amounts of sulfur dioxide into the atmosphere, which can react with sunlight, forming sulfuric acid aerosols that contribute to stunning sunsets and sunrises.

"The world's most explosive sound system!"

7. The volcanic island of Krakatoa in Indonesia experienced one of the most powerful eruptions in history in 1883. The explosion was so intense that it could be heard over 4,800 kilometers (3,000 miles) away.

8. Volcanoes can create their own weather patterns, such as volcanic thunderstorms, as intense heat and moisture interact with the volcanic plume.

9. Volcanic eruptions can result in the formation of new land masses. For example, the Hawaiian Islands were formed by volcanic activity over millions of years.

10. The deadliest volcanic eruption in the 20th century occurred in 1902 when Mount Pelée in Martinique erupted, destroying the town of Saint-Pierre and killing approximately 30,000 people.

11. When released in significant quantities, volcanic gas emissions, such as carbon dioxide and sulfur dioxide, can contribute to global warming and climate change.

"Where the floor is literally lava!"

12. Some volcanoes have a lava lake, a pool of molten lava within their crater. One notable example is Mount Nyiragongo in the Democratic Republic of the Congo.

13. Volcanic eruptions can trigger tsunamis when large amounts of material are rapidly displaced into the ocean, creating powerful waves.

Wildfires

1. Wildfires can generate their own weather systems, including fire whirls or "fire tornadoes," which can reach speeds of over 100 miles per hour.

   "Talk about a hot streak!"

2. The largest wildfire in recorded history occurred in 2019-2020 in Australia, known as the Black Summer bushfires, scorching an estimated 46 million acres.

3. A single wildfire can release more carbon dioxide into the atmosphere than several years of industrial emissions, exacerbating climate change.

4. Some tree species, like the lodgepole pine, rely on wildfires to release their seeds, as the intense heat opens their cones and allows for regeneration.

5. The United States experiences more wildfires than any other

The Environment

country, with an average of 70,000 wildfires burning over 7 million acres annually.

"Even lightning wants to play with fire!"

6. Lightning strikes cause a significant number of wildfires, responsible for about 10% of all ignitions in the United States.

7. Wildfires can create their own unique ecosystems, known as "pyrodiversity," where certain species thrive in fire-adapted habitats.

8. Smaller fires, called "spot fires," can be started by embers carried by the wind, causing new outbreaks and making wildfires more challenging to contain.

9. Some plants and trees, like the giant sequoias, have thick bark and high water content, which help protect them from the heat of wildfires.

"Climate change, the ultimate fire-starter!"

10. Climate change is expected to increase the frequency and intensity of wildfires as rising temperatures and changing weather patterns create more favorable conditions for fire ignition and spread.

11. Wildfires can impact air quality over vast distances, as smoke particles and pollutants can be carried by winds, affecting respiratory health in neighboring regions.

12. Certain animals, like birds of prey, take advantage of wildfires to find food more easily as the fire flushes out prey species.

13. Wildfires have the potential to cause significant soil erosion and impair water quality, as the loss of vegetation removes natural barriers and increases runoff.

14. Some firefighters use specially trained goats to create firebreaks by eating dry vegetation, reducing the available fuel for wildfires.

Ancient China

1. Ancient Chinese emperors were known to keep crickets as pets, often carrying them in tiny golden cages for good luck.

2. The Great Wall of China was not a continuous structure but a series of walls built and expanded over centuries by different dynasties.

3. Chinese paper money was invented during the Tang Dynasty, making China the first to use paper currency.

   "Chinese paper money: Tang-tastic innovation!"

4. Tea was discovered in ancient China and quickly became an integral part of Chinese culture, leading to the development of elaborate tea ceremonies.

5. The Chinese invented the compass during the Han Dynasty, revolutionizing navigation and exploration.

Ancient Civilizations

6. The ancient Chinese had a system of writing called the oracle bone script, which involved inscribing questions on animal bones and then interpreting the cracks that formed when heated.

7. The terracotta army, discovered in Xi'an, is a vast collection of life-sized clay soldiers buried with the first emperor of China to protect him in the afterlife.

8. The Silk Road, an ancient network of trade routes, connected China with the Middle East, Europe, and Africa, facilitating cultural exchange and economic growth.

"Gunpowder: from medicine to explosive surprises!"

9. The ancient Chinese invented gunpowder initially used for medicinal purposes before being developed into a weapon.

10. Foot binding was a practice in ancient China where women's feet were tightly bound to keep them small, representing beauty and social status.

11. The Chinese calendar is one of the oldest in the world and is based on lunar cycles, with each year represented by one of the 12 animals in the zodiac.

12. The Chinese were pioneers in agricultural practices, inventing the iron plow, seed drill, and water-powered mills, which greatly increased crop yields.

"Chess: ancient 'xiangqi,' checkmate strategies!"

13. Ancient Chinese astronomers made significant advancements in celestial observations and accurately predicted solar and lunar eclipses.

14. In ancient China, chess was invented as a military strategy game called "xiangqi," played on a checkered board with pieces representing different ranks of soldiers.

15. With its holistic approach, Chinese medicine dates back thousands of years and includes acupuncture, herbal remedies, and various therapeutic techniques.

Ancient Egypt

1. Ancient Egyptians considered the heart, not the brain, as the center of intelligence and emotions, believing it was essential for the afterlife.

2. Cats held sacred status in ancient Egypt and were worshipped as the embodiment of the goddess Bastet, often mummified and buried alongside their owners.

3. The Great Pyramid of Giza, built for Pharaoh Khufu, was the tallest man-made structure in the world for over 3,800 years until the construction of the Lincoln Cathedral in England.

4. The practice of embalming and mummification in ancient Egypt was not limited to humans; even animals like baboons, crocodiles, and falcons were mummified. *"Mummified animals: ancient Egyptian pet cemetery!"*

5. Ancient Egyptians had a remarkable knowledge of medicine

Ancient Civilizations

6. The pharaoh Tutankhamun, whose tomb was discovered nearly intact in 1922, was just a teenager when he ascended the throne and ruled Egypt for approximately nine years.

7. Egyptian hieroglyphs, a complex writing system, were deciphered in the early 19th century thanks to the Rosetta Stone, which contained the same text in three different scripts.

"Heart vs. feather: the original weigh-in!"

8. Ancient Egyptians believed in an elaborate afterlife, where the deceased's heart would be weighed against the feather of Ma'at, the goddess of truth, to determine their fate.

9. Beer played a significant role in ancient Egyptian culture, serving not only as a popular beverage but also as a form of currency and an offering to the gods.

10. The annual flooding of the Nile River was crucial for the prosperity of ancient Egypt, as it deposited fertile silt that enriched the soil and facilitated agricultural abundance.

11. Ancient Egyptians were avid lovers of board games. One of the most popular games was "Senet," played with a board resembling a modern-day backgammon set.

12. The construction of massive temples and monuments in ancient Egypt involved an immense workforce, including skilled craftsmen, farmers during the off-season, and even prisoners of war.

"Cleopatra: the Egyptian Greek-language trendsetter!"

13. Cleopatra VII, the last pharaoh of Egypt, was of Greek descent and the first ruler in her dynasty to speak Egyptian. She famously aligned herself with Julius Caesar and later Mark Antony.

Ancient Greece

1. Ancient Greeks considered left-handedness a sign of intelligence and creativity, so they revered left-handed individuals.

2. The Greeks practiced ostracism, a democratic process where citizens could vote to exile a fellow citizen for ten years.

3. The first-ever Olympic Games took place in 776 BCE and consisted of a single athletic event: a footrace.

4. Spartan women had more rights and freedom than their counterparts in other Greek city-states, and they could own property and receive education.

   "Spartan women: ahead of their time, literally!"

5. The Greeks believed that Zeus, the king of gods, directly influenced weather phenomena such as thunderstorms and lightning strikes.

Ancient Civilizations

6. Ancient Greeks used a water-powered clock called a clepsydra to measure time, with a float that marked the hours as it descended.

7. The Greeks had a word, "akrasia," to describe the state of acting against one's better judgment or succumbing to weakness.

8. Pythagoras, known for his famous theorem, also believed in the transmigration of souls, the idea that humans could be reborn in different forms.

9. The ancient Greeks strongly believed in the power and influence of dreams and considered them a means of communication with the gods.

"The Trojan War: history's greatest reality TV show!"

10. The Trojan War, which inspired Homer's epic poem "The Iliad," was likely a real historical event, although the details and extent remain debated.

11. The Greeks had a unique musical instrument called the hydraulis, an early organ version that used water pressure to produce sound.

12. The Greek philosopher Diogenes famously lived in a large ceramic jar to symbolize his rejection of material possessions and societal conventions.

"Onions and garlic: nature's performance-enhancing superfoods!"

13. Ancient Greeks had a custom called "ekphora," where they conducted processions and ceremonies to accompany the deceased to their final resting place.

14. Ancient Greek physicians believed certain foods, such as onions and garlic, could enhance physical performance and improve overall health.

15. The Greeks believed that speaking or writing a person's true name could give others power over them, so they often used pseudonyms.

Ancient India

"They really knew how to keep the streets clean!"

1. Ancient India had advanced urban planning, with cities like Mohenjo-Daro and Harappa having sophisticated drainage systems and well-organized streets.

2. The world's first recorded dockyard was found in Lothal, an ancient Indus Valley Civilization site in present-day Gujarat, India.

3. The concept of zero as a numerical digit was discovered in ancient India and later transmitted to the rest of the world.

4. India's ancient universities, such as Nalanda and Takshashila, attracted students worldwide and offered courses in various disciplines, including mathematics, astronomy, and medicine.

5. The iron pillar at the Qutub Minar complex in Delhi, built during the Gupta Empire, has stood for over 1,600 years

Ancient Civilizations

without rusting or corroding.

"They 'nailed' the number system!"

6. Ancient Indians developed the decimal system and the numerical notations used today, including the numeral symbols from 1 to 9 and the place value system.

7. The game of chess, known as "Chaturanga" in ancient India, was invented around the 6th century and spread to Persia, where it further evolved into modern chess.

8. The Kama Sutra, a famous ancient Indian text, is not solely about sexual positions but also explores human relationships, love, and societal norms.

"Their writing system was a real mystery!"

9. The Indus Valley Civilization, which thrived from around 3300 BCE to 1300 BCE, was one of the world's earliest urban civilizations and had a complex system of writing that remains undeciphered.

10. Ancient Indians were pioneers in medicine and surgical techniques, performing complex surgeries like cataract extraction, rhinoplasty, and even brain surgery.

11. The oldest known Sanskrit literature, the Rigveda, dates back to around 1500 BCE and is one of the oldest texts in any Indo-European language.

12. Ashoka, an emperor of the Maurya Empire, converted to Buddhism after witnessing the horrors of war and became a proponent of peace and non-violence.

13. Ancient India had a flourishing maritime trade network, with goods like spices, textiles, and precious stones being exported to distant lands like the Roman Empire and Southeast Asia.

14. The concept of non-violence and peaceful resistance, known as "ahimsa," was propagated by spiritual leaders like Mahavira and later adopted by Mahatma Gandhi during India's struggle for independence.

Ancient Rome

1. Roman gladiators were often trained as professional athletes, with some reaching celebrity status, but their average lifespan was shockingly short, typically ranging from 25 to 30 years.

2. The Romans had a complex and sophisticated system of underground aqueducts known as the Cloaca Maxima, which served to drain the city of Rome and carry away sewage.

3. The Colosseum, one of Rome's most iconic landmarks, had a retractable roof known as the "velarium" that could be opened or closed to provide shade for the spectators.

4. In ancient Rome, it was common for wealthy Romans to consume a meal while reclining on a couch rather than sitting at a table, a practice known as "lectus triclinaris."

5. The Roman Empire covered an enormous area, spanning three

"Dining in style: Roman couch potatoes!"

Ancient Civilizations

"Thermae: where cleanliness and socializing met!"

continents (Europe, Asia, and Africa), and at its height, it had a population estimated to be around 60 million people.

6. The Romans were pioneers in the field of concrete construction. They developed a type of concrete called "opus caementicium," which created large, durable structures like the Pantheon.

7. Roman women had more rights and freedoms compared to their counterparts in other ancient societies. They could own property, engage in business, and even divorce their husbands.

8. The Romans were avid bathers and believed in the therapeutic properties of bathing. Public baths, called "thermae," were integral to Roman social life.

"Roman numerals: letters gone numerical!"

9. Roman numerals, which are still used today, originated in ancient Rome. They were based on a system of letters, with each letter representing a specific value.

10. The Romans had a sophisticated system of road networks, collectively known as the "Viae Romanae," which spanned over 250,000 miles (400,000 km) and facilitated trade and military movements.

11. Ancient Romans used a form of central heating known as "hypocaust." This system involved pumping hot air through channels under the floors and walls of buildings.

12. The Romans were obsessed with hygiene and cleanliness. They would visit bathhouses daily, scrape their skin with a tool called a "strigil" to remove dirt and oils, and use perfumes to mask odors.

13. Roman emperors often employed food tasters, known as "punctatores," to ensure their meals were not poisoned.

14. The Romans were skilled engineers and architects. They constructed massive structures such as aqueducts, roads, and bridges, many of which still exist today.

Famous Composers

1. Wolfgang Amadeus Mozart, renowned for his prodigious talent, composed his first symphony at the age of 8, captivating audiences with his musical genius.

   "No hearing? No problem for Beethoven!"

2. Ludwig van Beethoven, a prolific composer, continued to create extraordinary masterpieces even after losing his hearing, proving that true artistry knows no boundaries.

3. Johann Sebastian Bach had a large family, with 20 children in total, including musicians and composers who inherited their father's musical abilities.

4. Franz Schubert, known for his beautiful melodies, composed over 600 songs in his short life, leaving an indelible mark on the world of classical music.

5. Clara Schumann, a remarkable pianist and composer, was also

Music

"Depression can't dim Tchaikovsky's musical brilliance!"

a devoted wife to Robert Schumann, managing his career and preserving his legacy.

6. Pyotr Ilyich Tchaikovsky, famous for his ballet scores, such as "Swan Lake" and "The Nutcracker," suffered from bouts of depression throughout his life.

7. Johann Strauss II, the "Waltz King," composed numerous beloved waltzes, including the iconic "The Blue Danube," which remains popular to this day.

8. Antonio Vivaldi, known for his Baroque compositions, was a priest and violin virtuoso, gaining fame for his concertos, particularly "The Four Seasons."

9. Franz Joseph Haydn, often called the "Father of the Symphony," composed over 100 symphonies, shaping the development of classical music.

10. George Frideric Handel's masterpiece, the oratorio "Messiah," was composed in just 24 days, demonstrating his incredible speed and creativity.

"Stravinsky: making music that causes a riot!"

11. Igor Stravinsky's ballet score, "The Rite of Spring," caused a riot during its premiere in 1913, as its avant-garde nature shocked and provoked the audience.

12. Giuseppe Verdi, one of the most celebrated opera composers, originally pursued a career in law before devoting himself entirely to music.

13. Richard Wagner, known for his epic operas, built his own opera house, the Bayreuth Festspielhaus, specifically designed to showcase his compositions.

14. Johannes Brahms, a perfectionist in his craft, destroyed many of his early compositions, striving for excellence and leaving only his finest works behind.

Musical Genres

"Rock and roll took a surprising turn!"

1. The term "rock and roll" was originally slang for sexual intercourse before it became associated with the popular music genre.

2. The origins of jazz can be traced back to New Orleans in the late 19th century, where African, European, and Caribbean musical traditions merged to create a unique style.

3. Classical music is often associated with Western tradition, but did you know there are also rich and diverse classical music traditions in other parts of the world, such as Indian classical music?

4. Reggae music, which originated in Jamaica, was heavily influenced by Rastafarianism, a religious and social movement that developed in the 1930s.

Music

"Hip-hop: the beat that speaks up!"

5. Hip-hop music, a genre born in the Bronx, New York, played a significant role in empowering marginalized communities and giving a voice to the unheard.

"EDM: the underground went global and wild!"

6. Electronic dance music (EDM) has its roots in the underground music scene of the 1970s, and it has since evolved into a global phenomenon with various subgenres like trance, house, and dubstep.

7. Country music, often associated with rural America, has a rich history that includes influences from Irish, Scottish, and English folk music.

8. The origins of the blues, a genre that has heavily influenced rock and roll, can be traced back to African American communities in the Southern United States in the late 19th century.

9. Salsa music, which originated in the Caribbean, particularly Cuba and Puerto Rico, fuses elements of Afro-Cuban rhythms with jazz and other genres.

10. Punk rock, known for its rebellious and do-it-yourself ethos, emerged in the 1970s as a reaction against the commercialization of mainstream music.

11. Bollywood music, a popular genre from the Indian film industry, incorporates various musical styles, from traditional Indian classical to Western pop and electronic sounds.

12. Opera, a grand and theatrical form of music, combines singing, acting, and orchestral accompaniment, often conveying powerful emotions and stories.

13. World music is a term used to describe a diverse range of musical styles and traditions from around the globe, highlighting our planet's richness and cultural diversity.

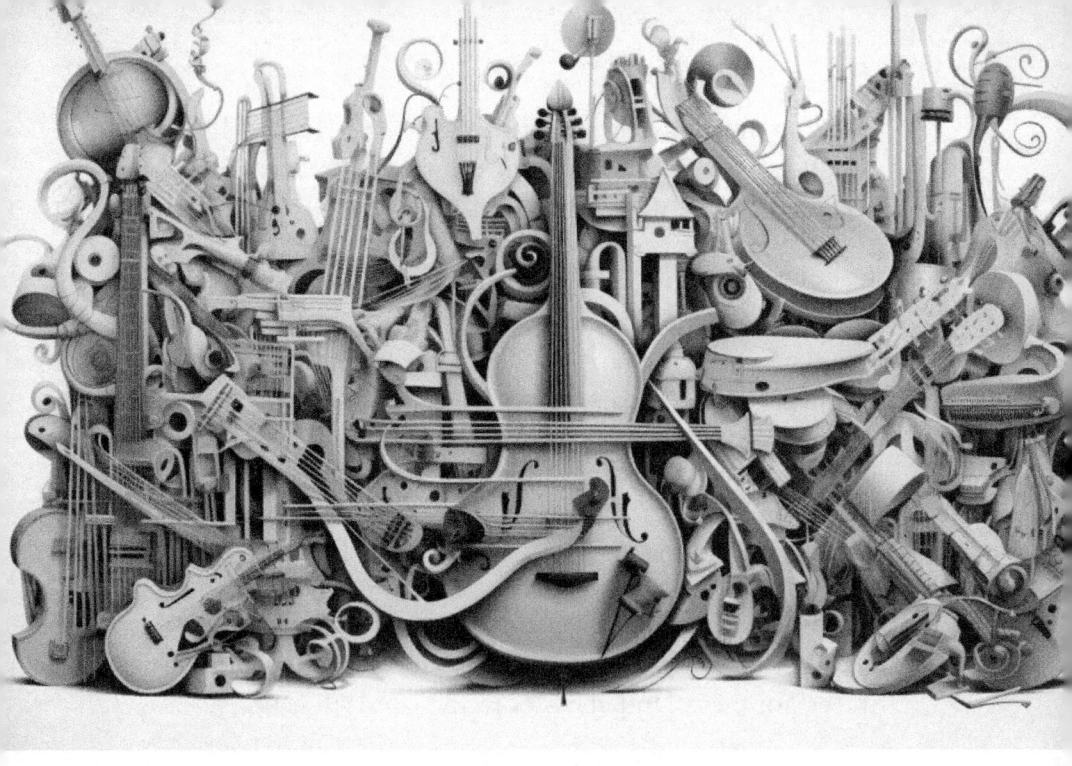

Musical Instruments

1. The glass harmonica, invented by Benjamin Franklin, uses glass bowls of different sizes to produce hauntingly beautiful melodies.

2. The Theremin, created by Leon Theremin in 1920, is the only musical instrument played without physical contact.

3. The kazoo, a small, buzzing instrument, was invented by Alabama Vest in the 1840s and gained popularity as a children's toy.

4. The octobass, a massive instrument standing over 11 feet tall, produces deep, resonant sounds and is rarely played due to its size.

5. The ocarina, a small wind instrument, dates back over 12,000 years and was found in ancient cultures worldwide.

"12,000 years of ocarina-playing expertise!"

Music

6. The Chapman Stick, developed by Emmett Chapman in 1969, is a unique string instrument that allows players to play bass and melody lines simultaneously.

"Be careful, the glass armonica might drive you mad!"

7. The glass armonica, invented by Benjamin Franklin, was a popular instrument in the 18th century, but its eerie sound led to superstitions about it causing madness.

8. The Hang drum, created in 2000, is a percussion instrument known for its melodic tones and unique UFO-like shape.

9. The serpent, a wind instrument resembling a twisted brass snake, was used extensively in European church music from the 16th to 19th centuries.

10. The musical saw, played by bending a saw blade and using a violin bow, produces an ethereal sound often associated with ghostly or haunting melodies.

"The musical saw: making ghosts jealous since forever!"

11. The Cristal Baschet, an avant-garde instrument invented in the 1950s, uses metal rods and glass rods to produce resonant, haunting sounds.

12. The ondes Martenot, an early electronic instrument invented in 1928, creates eerie and otherworldly tones through the use of vacuum tubes and a keyboard.

13. The hurdy-gurdy, a medieval string instrument, uses a crank and wheel to produce sound, creating a unique blend of strings and organ-like tones.

14. The musical saw, despite its unconventional nature, has been featured in various musical genres, including classical, folk, and even jazz.

15. The theremin's otherworldly sound can be heard in numerous film scores, including the classic sci-fi movie "The Day the Earth Stood Still."

World Currencies

1. The Indonesian rupiah is the currency with the highest denominations, with banknotes up to 100,000 rupiah.

2. The Maldivian currency, the Maldivian Rufiyaa, features a unique polymer banknote that is waterproof and resistant to tearing.

   "The Kuwaiti dinar: making dollars feel inferior!"

3. The Kuwaiti dinar is the world's highest-valued currency, with one dinar being equivalent to about three US dollars.

4. The Venezuelan bolívar has experienced extreme hyperinflation, to the point where higher denominations of millions and billions are necessary.

5. The Samoan tālā is one of the few currencies to feature non-circular coins with pentagonal and heptagonal shapes.

The World

6. The currency of Greenland, the Danish krone, is issued by the National Bank of Denmark and is also used in Denmark itself.

7. The Comorian franc, used in the Comoros Islands, is one of the few currencies that doesn't have any coins and is only available in banknotes.

"The Moroccan dirham: money with fancy calligraphy!"

8. The Moroccan dirham features a unique symbol, a stylized Arabic script representing the Arabic word "dirham."

9. The Japanese yen banknotes have braille markings to assist visually impaired individuals in identifying the denominations.

10. The Argentine peso underwent significant changes, including the replacement of its 1 peso coin with a note due to high inflation.

"The Cambodian riel: featuring the Temple of Dreams!"

11. The Cambodian riel is the only currency in the world to depict a building that does not exist—the Temple of Angkor Wat.

12. The Ghanaian cedi has different names for the various denominations, such as "sika" for the 1 cedi coin and "papa" for the 50 cedi note.

13. The Croatian kuna features a unique shape, with some coins having a wavy edge instead of the usual smooth circular edge.

14. The Bhutanese ngultrum is pegged to the Indian rupee at par value, which means they have an exchange rate of 1:1.

15. The currency of Malawi, the Malawian kwacha, is issued in both banknotes and plastic polymer banknotes, known as "plastic money."

16. The Israeli shekel is one of the few currencies that are not divisible into smaller units, with one shekel being the smallest denomination.

World Flags

1. The flag of Nepal is the only national flag that is not rectangular. It features two overlapping triangles representing the country's mountains.

2. The flag of Mozambique is the only national flag in the world to depict an AK-47 rifle, symbolizing the country's struggle for independence.

3. The Cyprus flag features the island's outline in copper color, representing its historical association with copper mining.

4. The flag of Vatican City is square in shape, mirroring the traditional shape of papal flags, distinguishing it from the rectangular flags of sovereign states.

   "Bhutan's got the most badass flag mascot!"

5. The flag of Bhutan features a dragon known as Druk, symbolizing the country's sovereignty and the thunder dragon

The World

6. The flag of Canada, also known as the Maple Leaf flag, was designed in a national flag competition and was officially adopted on February 15, 1965.

7. The flag of South Africa is one of the few national flags to contain six colors: black, green, yellow, white, red, and blue.

8. The flag of Denmark, known as the Dannebrog, is one of the oldest national flags in the world, with a design dating back to the 13th century.

"Jamaica: breaking the color code rules!"

9. The flag of Jamaica is the only national flag that does not contain any of the colors red, white, or blue.

10. The flag of Greece consists of nine alternating blue and white stripes representing the nine syllables of the Greek phrase "Eleftheria i Thanatos" (Freedom or Death).

11. The flag of India, adopted in 1947, features three horizontal bands of saffron, white, and green, with a blue chakra in the middle symbolizing progress.

12. The flag of Switzerland is square in shape and features a white cross on a red background, with the dimensions of the cross being defined precisely.

"Brazil's flag: a golden field of wealth!"

13. The flag of Brazil features a green field with a large yellow diamond representing the country's wealth in gold, and the blue circle symbolizes the sky.

14. The flag of Finland, also known as the "siniristilippu" or blue cross flag, symbolizes the country's lakes and forests with a blue Nordic cross on a white background.

15. The flag of Saudi Arabia consists of a green field with the Shahada (Islamic creed) written in white Arabic script and a sword on the upper hoist side.

World Maps

1. The world's oldest known map, the Babylonian Map of the World, dates back to the 6th century BCE and depicts the world as a flat disk.

   "Latitude and longitude for pinpointing awkward dates!"

2. The Ptolemaic maps of the 2nd century CE introduced the concept of latitude and longitude lines, allowing for more accurate representations of the world.

3. The famous Mercator projection, developed by Gerardus Mercator in 1569, distorts the size of landmasses, making countries closer to the poles appear much larger.

4. The Peters projection, created by Arno Peters in 1974, aimed to address the distortion of the Mercator projection by accurately representing the relative sizes of countries.

5. The largest printed world map, known as the "Earth Platinum,"

The World

"Google loves distortions, but we forgive them!"

    measures a staggering 12 feet by 6 feet and was created by Australian geographer Stuart McArthur in 2007.

6. Despite its distortions, the world map used by Google Maps and many other online mapping services is based on the Mercator projection.

7. The Gall-Peters projection, introduced in 1855, is another attempt at more accurately representing landmasses' sizes, but it sacrifices shape accuracy.

8. The Mappa Mundi, a medieval map created around 1300 CE, depicts Jerusalem as the center of the world, with Europe, Asia, and Africa surrounding it.

9. The Waldseemüller map, produced in 1507, was the first to label the newly discovered continent of America after Amerigo Vespucci, who recognized it as a new landmass.

"Triangles: nature's way of balancing landmasses!"

10. The "Butterfly Map" by Bernard J.S. Cahill in 1909 aimed to provide a more balanced representation of the Earth's landmasses by dividing the globe into equal-area triangles.

11. The AuthaGraph World Map, designed by Hajime Narukawa in 2016, attempts to minimize distortion by using a complex system of 96 triangles to create a nearly accurate representation.

12. Many early maps included sea monsters, mythical creatures, and unexplored territories as decorative elements, reflecting the limited knowledge and imagination of the time.

13. The "Upside-Down Map" flips the world map, with the south at the top, challenging the conventional Eurocentric perspective.

14. The Dymaxion map, created by Buckminster Fuller in 1943, presents the world on a modified icosahedron, allowing for less distortion and easy folding.

World Oceans

1. The Pacific Ocean, covering more than 63 million square miles, is the world's largest ocean, accounting for approximately one-third of the Earth's surface.

2. The Mariana Trench in the Pacific is the deepest part of any ocean, plunging to a staggering depth of about 36,000 feet.

3. The Arctic Ocean is the smallest and shallowest ocean, but it houses the North Pole and remains covered by ice for most of the year.

4. The Atlantic Ocean is expanding at a rate of about an inch per year due to the movement of tectonic plates.

"Winds playing tricks, nature's got jokes!"

5. The Indian Ocean is home to a unique natural phenomenon called the "Maldive Islands Reverse Monsoon," where winds reverse direction during certain times of the year.

"Chilly ocean, bring a sweater!"

6. The Southern Ocean, also known as the Antarctic Ocean, surrounds Antarctica and has the coldest average temperature of any ocean.

7. The Red Sea, located between Africa and Asia, got its name due to the presence of a type of algae that gives the water a reddish tint.

8. The Caribbean Sea is known for its vibrant coral reefs, including the Great Barrier Reef, the largest coral reef system in the world.

9. The Mediterranean Sea, known for its rich history, was once a dry basin millions of years ago before it was filled by the Atlantic Ocean.

"Baltic Sea: the ocean's low-sodium option!"

10. The Baltic Sea is unique because it has a lower salt concentration compared to other oceans due to its connection to several freshwater rivers.

11. The Gulf of Mexico, bordered by the United States and Mexico, experiences frequent hurricane activity, often causing significant damage to coastal areas.

12. The Andaman Sea, located in Southeast Asia, is home to several remote and uninhabited islands, including the popular tourist destination of Phuket.

13. The Tasman Sea, separating Australia and New Zealand, is named after the Dutch explorer Abel Tasman, the first European to navigate it in the 17th century.

14. The Coral Sea, situated off the northeastern coast of Australia, is renowned for its diverse marine life and stunning coral reefs.

15. The Bering Sea, located between Alaska and Russia, experiences extreme temperature variations, with freezing temperatures in winter and milder conditions in summer.

World Records

1. The fastest time to type the alphabet on a touchscreen device is a mere 3.47 seconds, achieved by Gaurav Sharma in 2018.

2. The world record for the most tattoos in 24 hours by a single person was set by Hollis Cantrell in 2008, who completed an astounding 801 tattoos.

   "Talk about a never-ending tennis match!"

3. The longest tennis match in history took place in 2010 and lasted for 11 hours and 5 minutes, with John Isner defeating Nicolas Mahut.

4. Ashrita Furman holds the record for the most Guinness World Records titles, with over 200 records to his name.

5. The largest gathering of people dressed as penguins occurred in 2015 when 624 participants donned penguin costumes in London.

The World

6. The longest distance skateboarding in 24 hours is 720.8 km (447.01 miles), achieved by Joe Briceno in 2021.

7. The world's largest collection of rubber ducks is owned by Charlotte Lee, who amassed over 10,000 rubber ducks of various sizes and colors.

8. The longest successful basketball shot measured an astonishing 109.8 meters (360 feet, 10 inches) and was made by Thunder Law in 2016.

9. The world record for the most consecutive push-ups is 10,507, achieved by Minoru Yoshida in 1980.

10. The fastest time to solve a Rubik's Cube using only one hand is 6.82 seconds, achieved by Feliks Zemdegs in 2018.

11. The largest gathering of people dressed as superheroes took place in 2015, with 1,580 participants dressed as their favorite comic book characters.

"That's some serious chin strength!"

12. The longest time balancing a guitar on the chin is 7 hours, 1 minute, and 25 seconds, achieved by Jonathan Finch in 2014.

13. The world's largest collection of traffic cones is owned by David Morgan, who has amassed over 137 different cones of various shapes and sizes.

14. The highest number of balloons burst using a laser beam in one minute is 100, achieved by Ashrita Furman in 2020.

"A hug that never seemed to end!"

15. The longest hug recorded lasted for 36 hours and was accomplished by Ron O'Neil and Theresa Kerr in 2010.

16. The largest human mattress dominoes involved 2,016 participants and took place in 2012 in New Orleans.

17. The highest skydive without a parachute was made by Luke Aikins in 2016 from a height of 7,620 meters (25,000 feet).

World Time Zones

1. The International Date Line, located in the Pacific Ocean, is where one day ends and the next begins, creating a 24-hour time difference.

2. Kiribati's Line Islands, including Kiritimati, are the first places on Earth to see the sunrise each day.

3. China follows a single time zone despite its vast size, resulting in significant variations in daylight hours across the country.

   "China: One country, one snooze button!"

4. Nepal has a unique time zone offset of 45 minutes ahead of Coordinated Universal Time (UTC), setting it apart from neighboring countries.

5. In Antarctica, some research stations use their own time zones, leading to an interesting mix of clocks within the continent.

The World

6. Several regions worldwide use unofficial or alternative time zones for historical or cultural reasons.

7. The Chatham Islands in New Zealand have a time zone offset of 45 minutes ahead of the mainland, making it the country's first to enter the new day.

8. Alaska observes four time zones, making it the U.S. state with the most time zones.

9. The concept of time zones was introduced in the late 19th century to facilitate efficient railway scheduling.

"Benjamin Franklin: The original clock-wrecker!"

10. The concept of Daylight Saving Time, adjusting the clock forward in the summer months, was first proposed by Benjamin Franklin in 1784.

11. Some countries, like Iran, have half-hour offsets, deviating from the usual one-hour increments commonly seen in time zones.

12. The time zone of Samoa changed in 2011, skipping December 30th entirely, to align itself with its neighboring countries in the Pacific.

"GMT, the has-been of time standards!"

13. The small country of Nepal, located between India and China, is home to a time zone that is 5 hours and 45 minutes ahead of Coordinated Universal Time (UTC+5:45).

14. The Greenwich Mean Time (GMT) was once used as the international time standard but has been largely replaced by Coordinated Universal Time (UTC).

15. North Korea created its own unique time zone in 2015, setting their clocks back by 30 minutes to mark the 70th anniversary of Korean independence from Japan.

16. The concept of time zones was first proposed by Sir Sandford Fleming, a Canadian engineer, in the late 19th century.

Black Lives Matter

1. Black Lives Matter (BLM) was founded in 2013 by Alicia Garza, Patrisse Cullors, and Opal Tometi after the acquittal of Trayvon Martin's killer.

    "From hashtag to hero!"

2. The hashtag #BlackLivesMatter was created by Alicia Garza as a call to action following George Zimmerman's acquittal.

3. BLM chapters exist worldwide, extending beyond the United States to places like Canada, the UK, Australia, and South Africa.

4. In 2016, BLM was nominated for the Nobel Peace Prize, recognizing its global impact on civil rights and racial justice.

5. BLM organizes using decentralized leadership, enabling grassroots movements to address local issues effectively.

"Fighting for justice, one fist at a time."

6. BLM advocates for justice and equality for Black people, addressing systemic racism, police brutality, and social injustice.

7. The movement inspired a significant increase in voter registration and civic engagement among marginalized communities.

8. BLM has been influential in prompting discussions about racial bias in media representation and cultural narratives.

9. The raised fist, a symbol of solidarity and resistance, has become synonymous with the Black Lives Matter movement.

10. The movement emphasizes intersectionality, recognizing how race intersects with other forms of discrimination.

11. In response to criticism, some counter-movements like "Blue Lives Matter" emerged, defending law enforcement.

12. BLM has inspired art, music, and literature that reflects the struggles and resilience of Black communities.

"Breaking barriers, one share at a time."

13. Patrisse Cullors' book "When They Call You a Terrorist" recounts her experiences as a BLM co-founder and activist.

14. Social media played a crucial role in amplifying BLM's message, allowing it to reach a global audience.

15. BLM advocates for the defunding of police departments and reallocating resources to community services.

16. Despite facing criticism, BLM has continued to advocate for racial justice through peaceful protests and advocacy.

17. The Black Lives Matter movement remains a significant force, continuously striving for a more inclusive and equitable society.

COVID-19

"Thanks a lot, 2020. Wuhan, really?"

1. COVID-19, caused by the SARS-CoV-2 virus, was first identified in Wuhan, China, in December 2019 and quickly spread globally.

2. The virus primarily spreads through respiratory droplets when an infected person coughs, sneezes, talks, or breathes heavily.

3. COVID-19 can survive on surfaces like plastic and stainless steel for up to three days, increasing the risk of transmission.

4. Research suggests that the virus can also spread through aerosols, which are tiny particles that can remain suspended in the air.

5. Some studies indicate that COVID-19 may survive in the air for a few hours under certain conditions.

Social Topics

"Older adults playing the real-life 'Groundhog Day!"

6. COVID-19 can affect people of all ages, but older adults and those with underlying health conditions are at a higher risk of severe illness and complications.

7. While most individuals experience mild to moderate symptoms, some can develop severe pneumonia, acute respiratory distress syndrome (ARDS), or organ failure.

8. COVID-19 can cause a range of symptoms, including fever, cough, shortness of breath, loss of taste or smell, fatigue, and body aches.

9. Loss of smell, known as anosmia, has been reported as one of the early and distinct symptoms of COVID-19.

"The invisible ninja strikes again!"

10. Asymptomatic individuals can still transmit the virus, making it challenging to control its spread effectively.

11. COVID-19 has a relatively long incubation period, ranging from 1 to 14 days, with an average of around 5-6 days.

12. Some studies suggest that certain blood types, such as type A, may be more susceptible to severe illness, while type O might have some protection.

13. Long COVID, or post-acute sequelae of SARS-CoV-2 infection (PASC), refers to symptoms that persist or develop after the acute phase of the illness.

14. The virus can potentially affect multiple organs, including the lungs, heart, kidneys, brain, and gastrointestinal system.

15. COVID-19 can trigger an exaggerated immune response known as a cytokine storm, leading to widespread inflammation and severe illness.

16. Research indicates that the virus mutates over time, with various variants emerging, some of which are more transmissible or may affect vaccine efficacy.

North Korea

1. North Korea operates the world's deepest metro system in Pyongyang, with stations built deep underground to serve as bomb shelters.

2. The country has its own calendar called the Juche calendar, which starts from the birth of North Korea's founding leader, Kim Il-sung.

3. North Korea has a state-approved hairstyle list for men and women, and citizens are required to choose from a limited set of government-approved styles.

"The internet: limited edition for elites!"

4. In an attempt to discourage foreign influence, North Korea strictly controls access to the internet, allowing only a limited number of people to have access.

5. The world's largest stadium, the Rungrado 1st of May Stadium,

Social Topics

"A game of loyalty and hairstyles!"

is in Pyongyang and can hold up to 114,000 spectators.

6. North Korea has a unique classification system for its citizens known as the "songbun," which categorizes individuals based on their loyalty to the regime.

7. According to state media, Kim Jong-il, the former leader of North Korea, was said to have scored 11 holes-in-one during his first-ever round of golf.

8. In an effort to maintain purity, North Korea strictly controls the introduction of foreign films, music, and literature into the country.

"When North Korea says 'No Windows'!"

9. North Korea operates its own operating system called Red Star OS, a modified version of Linux used for domestic purposes.

10. North Korea has its own version of the Internet, a state-controlled network called Kwangmyong, which offers limited access to approved websites and content.

11. The country operates a "Three Generations of Punishment" system, which can punish not only the offender but also their entire family for perceived crimes against the state.

12. North Korea has a massive underground tunnel network spanning hundreds of kilometers, designed for military purposes and potential invasion scenarios.

13. The government employs an elite group of hackers known as Bureau 121, who are believed responsible for cyberattacks on foreign targets.

14. North Korea operates the world's tallest unoccupied building, the Ryugyong Hotel, which stands at 330 meters high in Pyongyang.

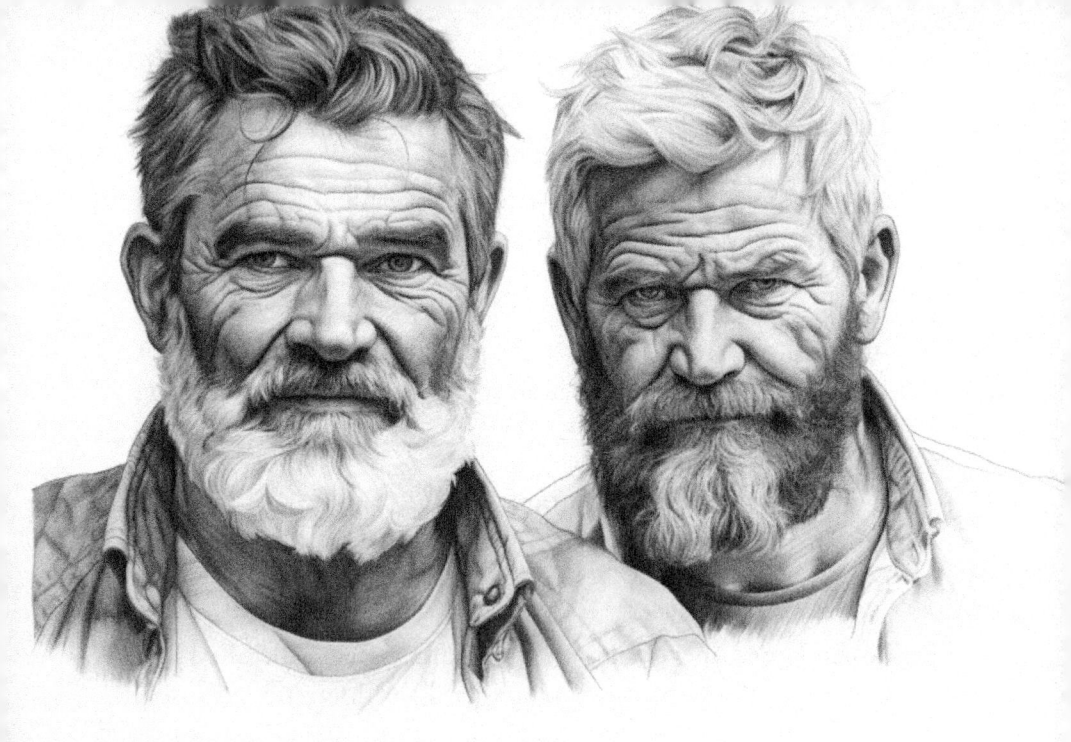

Amazing Coincidences

1. In 1980, Jim Lewis and Jim Springer discovered they were identical twins separated at birth, and both had married women named Linda.

   "Talk about a fictional foreshadowing!"

2. The Titanic disaster in 1912 had an eerie coincidence with the 1898 novel "Futility," as both described a massive ship sinking after hitting an iceberg.

3. In 1975, Erskine Lawrence Ebbin, a taxi driver, was killed by a taxi while crossing a street in Bermuda. The taxi's passenger? Erskine Lawrence Ebbin.

4. The assassination of Archduke Franz Ferdinand in 1914 coincidentally occurred on the same date as an unsuccessful assassination attempt on his life one year earlier.

5. In 1965, Paul Collins and Joseph Belanger, two separate

Miscellaneous

motorcyclists, collided with each other and died in a head-on collision while racing to the same location.

"A heart-stopping discovery, quite literally!"

6. The legendary composer, Frédéric Chopin, died in 1849 in Paris, and his heart was preserved in a jar. In 1945, the jar was discovered intact during World War II.

7. The novels "Fahrenheit 451" by Ray Bradbury and "1984" by George Orwell were both published in 1953, coincidentally foreseeing dystopian societies.

8. During the filming of "The Wizard of Oz" in 1939, the actor playing the Tin Man, Buddy Ebsen, had to be replaced due to an allergic reaction to the aluminum makeup.

9. In 1950, two female strangers named Linda and Charlie from the United States were aboard the same flight, discovered they had the same birthday, and both lived on Baker Street.

10. The iconic scientist, Isaac Newton, was born on December 25, 1642, the same day Galileo Galilei died, both regarded as pioneers in the field of physics.

"From inmate to mayor, talk about a plot twist!"

11. A remarkable coincidence happened in 2002 when a man named Richard Parker was elected mayor of a town in Missouri, despite being in prison for murder.

12. In 1909, a boy named George Burks took a photograph of his childhood friend, Jack Robinson. Years later, they discovered they were brothers who had been separated at birth.

13. On November 8, 1970, a Japanese man named Tsutomu Yamaguchi survived the atomic bomb in Hiroshima. Three days later, he was in Nagasaki when the second bomb struck.

14. In 1940, the renowned psychoanalyst Carl Jung experienced vivid dreams about Europe being destroyed by a catastrophic flood, coinciding with the outbreak of World War II.

Mathematics and Numbers

1. The number zero was not widely recognized in Europe until the 12th century, despite its existence in ancient civilizations like the Mayans and Babylonians.

   "23 million digits? That's prime time!"

2. The largest known prime number, discovered in 2018, has a staggering 23,249,425 digits. Prime numbers have fascinated mathematicians for centuries.

3. The golden ratio, approximately 1.6180339887, is a mathematical constant that appears in nature, art, and architecture, creating aesthetically pleasing proportions.

4. The number pi (π), which represents the ratio of a circle's circumference to its diameter, is an irrational number, meaning it cannot be expressed as a finite fraction.

5. Gödel's incompleteness theorems, formulated by mathematician

Miscellaneous

"Size matters, even in infinity!"

Kurt Gödel in 1931, demonstrated that no consistent system of mathematics can prove its own consistency.

6. The concept of infinity has different sizes. The cardinality of the set of natural numbers is "countable" infinity, while real numbers have a "larger" uncountable infinity.

"Banach-Tarski: the ultimate magic trick!"

7. The Banach-Tarski paradox, established in 1924, shows that a solid ball can be divided into a finite number of pieces that can be rearranged to form two identical copies of the original ball.

8. The Four Color Theorem states that any map on a plane can be colored using only four colors, with no two adjacent regions having the same color.

9. The Fibonacci sequence, where each number is the sum of the two preceding numbers (1, 1, 2, 3, 5, 8, 13, ...), appears in nature, such as the arrangement of sunflower seeds or pinecone spirals.

10. The number 1729 is known as the Hardy-Ramanujan number. It may seem unremarkable, but mathematician Srinivasa Ramanujan found it interesting due to its unique properties.

11. The Möbius strip is a surface with only one side and one edge. If you cut it in half lengthwise, you end up with two linked and interlocked loops.

12. The Monty Hall problem, a probability puzzle, demonstrates that switching your choice in a game show can increase your chances of winning a prize.

13. The concept of zero is attributed to the ancient Indian mathematician Brahmagupta, who first defined and used it in mathematical equations in the 7th century.

Mythical Creatures

1. The Bonnacon, a creature from medieval bestiaries, defended itself by spraying a highly flammable substance from its rear end.

2. The Phoenix, a legendary bird, was believed to be reborn from its own ashes, symbolizing eternal life and resurrection.

3. The Manticore, a mythical beast with the body of a lion, the tail of a scorpion, and the face of a human, originated from Persian mythology.

4. According to Scottish folklore, Kelpies were shape-shifting water spirits that took the form of horses and lured humans to their watery demise.

5. The Chupacabra, popular in Latin American folklore, is a vampire-like creature said to suck the blood of livestock.

"Chupacabra: the ultimate vampire mooch!"

Miscellaneous

6. In Slavic mythology, the Domovoi was a household spirit who protected the home and its occupants but could also be mischievous if offended.

7. The Ammit, a creature from ancient Egyptian mythology, had the head of a crocodile, the front legs of a lion, and the hind legs of a hippopotamus.

"Tengu: the original feathered martial artists!"

8. According to Japanese folklore, the Tengu were supernatural creatures with bird-like features and were known for their martial arts skills.

9. The Aswang, a creature from Filipino folklore, was believed to be a shapeshifting vampire-like creature that preyed on unborn children.

"Kitsune: sly foxes with PhDs in mischief!"

10. From Japanese mythology, the Kitsune were fox spirits capable of shape-shifting and possessing immense intelligence and magical powers.

11. The Jackalope, a creature from American folklore, was described as a hare with antelope-like antlers and was known for its elusive nature.

12. The Selkie, found in Scottish and Irish folklore, were seals that could shed their skin and transform into beautiful humans on land.

13. The Hodag, a legendary creature from Wisconsin, was said to have spikes along its back, large teeth, and the ability to emit foul-smelling smoke.

14. The Kraken, a colossal sea monster from Nordic folklore, was said to dwell in the ocean's depths and terrorize sailors.

15. The Yara-ma-yha-who, an Australian Aboriginal creature, had a red mouth, no teeth, and could swallow humans whole before regurgitating them.

Strange Phobias

1. Xanthophobia is the fear of the color yellow. It can cause anxiety, panic attacks, and avoidance of yellow objects or environments.

2. Pogonophobia is the fear of beards. This phobia can stem from a traumatic experience or a fear of germs.

3. Chorophobia is the fear of dancing. Individuals with this phobia may feel uncomfortable or anxious in social situations involving dancing.

    "Keep your knees out of sight, alright?"

4. Genuphobia is the fear of knees. It may manifest as a fear of seeing or touching knees, or even a fear of one's own knees.

5. Ablutophobia is the fear of bathing or washing. People with this phobia may experience extreme anxiety or avoidance of personal hygiene practices.

Miscellaneous

6. Ombrophobia is the fear of rain. It can lead to heightened anxiety during rainfall or a strong aversion to rain exposure.

7. Nomophobia is the fear of being without a mobile phone or losing cellular signal. It is a modern phobia related to technology dependence.

"Feathered tickles? Not my cup of tea!"

8. Pteronophobia is the fear of being tickled by feathers. Individuals with this phobia may experience discomfort or anxiety around feathers or feather-like objects.

9. Chronophobia is the fear of time or the passing of time. It can manifest as anxiety about deadlines, schedules, or aging.

10. Allodoxaphobia is the fear of opinions. People with this phobia may fear expressing their opinions or hearing differing viewpoints.

"Don't worry, the ducks are quacking!"

11. Anatidaephobia is the fear that somewhere, somehow, a duck is watching you. It is an irrational fear that can cause significant distress.

12. Turophobia is the fear of cheese. Individuals with this phobia may feel anxious or repulsed by the sight, smell, or taste of cheese.

13. Phobophobia is the fear of developing a phobia. It is characterized by excessive worry and anxiety about experiencing or acquiring new phobias.

14. Linonophobia is the fear of string. It can cause individuals to avoid string-like objects, such as ropes, cords, or shoelaces.

15. Trypophobia is the fear of clusters of small holes or bumps. It can evoke intense anxiety, disgust, or discomfort in affected individuals.

Unexplained Disappearances

1. The Bermuda Triangle is infamous for unexplained disappearances, but did you know similar phenomena occur in other locations like the Bennington Triangle in Vermont?

2. The Sodder Children disappearance is a baffling case where five children vanished during a house fire in West Virginia in 1945. Their fate remains unknown.

3. In 1978, Frederick Valentich, an Australian pilot, disappeared while flying over the Bass Strait. Before vanishing, he reported an unidentified flying object hovering above him.

    "Australian pilot's close encounter with vanishing!"

4. The case of Ettore Majorana, an Italian physicist, is shrouded in mystery. He vanished without a trace in 1938, and his fate remains unknown to this day.

5. The Mary Celeste, an American merchant ship, was found

Miscellaneous

abandoned in 1872. The crew's disappearance remains unexplained, as no signs of foul play or piracy were found.

6. In 1947, Flight 19, a group of five U.S. Navy aircraft, vanished over the Bermuda Triangle during a training exercise. The disappearance sparked numerous theories.

7. The Roanoke Colony in North Carolina disappeared in the late 16th century, leaving behind only the word "Croatoan" carved into a tree, a mystery that has puzzled historians.

"Prime Minister takes a swim... forever!"

8. Harold Holt, the Prime Minister of Australia, disappeared while swimming in 1967. Despite extensive searches, his body was never found, leading to theories of foul play or abduction.

9. The Yuba County Five, a group of young men, disappeared after attending a basketball game in California in 1978. Their abandoned car was found, but their fate remains unknown.

10. In 1922, the Arctic explorer and aviator Roald Amundsen disappeared during a flight to rescue a missing crewmember. The wreckage was never found, leaving his fate a mystery.

11. The case of D.B. Cooper is one of the most famous unsolved disappearances. In 1971, he hijacked a plane, received a ransom, and parachuted away, never to be seen again.

"They must have lighthouse keep-away skills!"

12. The Flannan Isles Lighthouse mystery involves the unexplained disappearance of three lighthouse keepers in 1900. The only clue was an unfinished meal and the absence of the men.

13. The Lake Anjikuni mystery centers around an entire Inuit village in Canada that vanished overnight in 1930, leaving behind empty houses and missing inhabitants.

14. In 1966, Australian schoolgirls, known as the Beaumont children, disappeared while visiting a beach. Despite an extensive search, they were never found, haunting the nation ever since.

Unknown Movie Facts

1. In the movie "Titanic," the water used in the freezing scenes was actually heated for the comfort of the actors.

2. The iconic line "Here's Johnny!" from "The Shining" was improvised by Jack Nicholson during filming.

   "Turtles mating for dinosaur sound effects? Hilarious!"

3. During the "Jurassic Park" production, the dinosaur sounds were created by mixing animal noises, including turtles mating.

4. The character of E.T. was originally going to be a terrifying alien, but Steven Spielberg decided to make him more lovable.

5. The film "The Shawshank Redemption" initially had a disappointing box office performance but became a beloved classic through word of mouth.

6. The opening scene of "Saving Private Ryan" was shot in

Miscellaneous

> "Leo's 'king of the world' ad-lib rocks!"

sequence, and many of the extras had never seen a battle scene before to capture their genuine reactions.

7. The iconic "I'm the king of the world!" line from "Titanic" was ad-libbed by Leonardo DiCaprio during filming.

8. In "The Wizard of Oz," the Horse of a Different Color was actually painted with Jell-O powder to achieve its vibrant appearance.

9. The visual effects team for "The Matrix" created a custom-made camera rig called "Bullet Time" to capture the iconic slow-motion sequences.

10. The Lord of the Rings trilogy holds the record for the most Academy Awards won by a film franchise, with a total of 17 wins.

> "Leave the spinning top to audience debates!"

11. The spinning top at the end of "Inception" was intentionally left ambiguous to leave the interpretation of the film's ending to the audience.

12. The horror film "Psycho" was the first to show a toilet flushing on-screen, breaking a cinematic taboo.

13. The spaceship sound effects in "Star Wars" were created by recording the hum of an old projector motor mixed with other sounds.

14. The famous shower scene in "Psycho" consists of 78 different camera setups and 52 cuts in just under 3 minutes.

15. The cult classic "The Rocky Horror Picture Show" initially flopped at the box office but gained a dedicated following through midnight screenings.

16. The iconic "May the Force be with you" line from "Star Wars" has become a popular catchphrase, transcending the film's original context.

Unsolved Mysteries

1. The Voynich Manuscript, a 15th-century book written in an unknown language, has confounded codebreakers and linguists for centuries, defying all attempts at decipherment.

2. The disappearance of Malaysia Airlines Flight 370 in 2014 remains a baffling mystery, with no conclusive evidence or explanation regarding the fate of the aircraft and its passengers.

3. The Bermuda Triangle, an area in the western part of the North Atlantic Ocean, has been associated with numerous unexplained disappearances of ships and aircraft.

   "Jack the Ripper: the ultimate hide-and-seek champion!"

4. The identity of Jack the Ripper, the infamous serial killer who terrorized London in the late 1800s, has never been definitively established, leaving his true identity shrouded in mystery.

5. The Tunguska event of 1908, which caused a massive explosion

Miscellaneous

in a remote region of Siberia, is believed to have been caused by a meteorite or comet, but its exact nature remains uncertain.

"Those ancient Peruvians were giant doodlers!"

6. The Nazca Lines, enormous geoglyphs etched into the desert floor of Peru, continue to puzzle researchers due to their purpose and the methods by which they were created.

7. The fate of the lost colony of Roanoke, a group of settlers who vanished without a trace from present-day North Carolina in the late 16th century, has never been definitively solved.

8. The origins and purpose of Stonehenge, the prehistoric monument in England composed of massive standing stones, remain a subject of debate and speculation among archaeologists.

"The Zodiac Killer: master of hide and seek!"

9. The identity of the Zodiac Killer, a serial murderer active in Northern California during the late 1960s and early 1970s, has never been conclusively determined, leaving his crimes unsolved.

10. The Antikythera mechanism, an ancient Greek analog computer discovered in a shipwreck, remains a remarkable mystery, as its exact function and construction methods are still not fully understood.

11. The Dyatlov Pass incident, where nine experienced hikers died under mysterious circumstances in the Ural Mountains in 1959, continues to generate theories ranging from avalanches to paranormal activity.

12. The disappearance of the USS Cyclops, a Navy cargo ship in 1918, is one of the biggest non-combat losses of the U.S. Navy, and the cause remains unknown to this day.

13. The Wow! signal, detected in 1977, is a strong narrowband radio signal from space that has never been satisfactorily explained and has not been detected again since.

About the Author

Max Mercury is a certified "Fact-O-Holic" who thrives on exploring the bizarre and uncharted territories of knowledge. From a young age, Max developed an insatiable curiosity that led to countless adventures and a rather extensive collection of fun facts.

Legend has it that Max was born with a miniature library in hand and a twinkle in the eye that could detect fascinating facts from miles away. As a child, Max's bedroom was a treasure trove of encyclopedias, atlases, and stacks of peculiar books that would make even the most inquisitive minds green with envy.

Max's pursuit of facts took him to the most peculiar corners of the world. From scaling mountains to plumbing the depths of the deepest oceans, there was no fact too wild or too outlandish for Max to unearth. He even befriended a chatty parrot named Professor Squawkington, who could recite trivia about ancient civilizations in five different languages!

As an adult, Max's passion for facts only grew stronger. He became an official member of the "Fact Fanatics Society," an elite group of knowledge enthusiasts who dedicate their lives to uncovering the most mind-boggling tidbits of information. Max's reputation as a fact connoisseur grew, and soon people began referring to him as the "Curator of Curiosities."

Max's journey to compile *"1600+ Fascinating Facts!"* was not an easy one. It involved countless hours of research, late-night debates with fellow fact enthusiasts, and the occasional accidental fact explosion (fortunately, Max had a fire extinguisher handy). But the result is a collection of facts that will amaze, entertain, and leave you in a constant state of awe.

Whether you're a seasoned fact aficionado or just starting your journey into the world of wonder, Max Mercury's *"1600+ Fascinating Facts!"* is your ticket to a mind-expanding experience like no other. So fasten your seatbelt, buckle up your brain, and get ready to embark on an unforgettable adventure with Max and his wondrous world of knowledge!

Inspire Our Next Edition

Congratulations, fellow knowledge seekers, you've just survived a rollercoaster ride through over 1600 mind-boggling facts! But hold on to your thinking caps, because the fun doesn't end here!

We're already brewing the secret sauce for our next fact-packed extravaganza, and we need YOUR help to spice up our next topics and chapters!

Send your hilarious, bizarre, and mind-blowing suggestions to info@cleverclickpress.com and be part of the wild journey into the heart of astonishing knowledge!

Remember, in the realm of facts, there's always room for more quirkiness! Let's conquer the world of curiosity together!

Printed in Great Britain
by Amazon